ENDORSEMEN

A story of Abrahamic faith, written as it was lived—in a mother's breathless desperation, and ultimately, her triumph and gratitude stronger than words. Christina Custodio holds the conviction children are on loan from God. Her journey with her son, Isaiah, reminds us of the power in such surrender. This book is a lifeline for anyone groping for faith in the dark. Christina shuns the Pollyanna cliche of so much faith prose, sticking instead to the essence of suffering and believing. In Hebrew her son's very name reminds us of the generosity of God. Their story does the very same. Her telling of it—a veritable thank-you note sent into the universe, and an updraft to us all.

—Michael Cogdill, father, author, Emmy winner

A mother's nightmare finds God's hope. From the moment I read the first line of Christina's book, I was pulled into her story. I found myself unable to put the book down, because I had to see what happened next. Christina opens the door to her fears, pain, hopes, joy and struggles on a journey no mother wants to ever go on. She allows us into the daily life of loving and caring for her son. Can we see God at work in the hopeless circumstances of life? Christina answers this question, and the answer is "YES!"

—Carole Leathem, speaker, author, *Finding Joy in My Messy Life*

Tears flowed with moments of gentle laughter as the tragedy of Isaiah's life found its way to victory. A story of hope expressed within the battle raging in a mother's fight to believe that God is enough. Told with raw emotion and wit, Christina's story will remind you that miracles still happen in our modern day world. So, settle in to embrace a reason to believe that God can take impossible to possible through the faith of this precious mama as an earthly kingdom is shaken for His glory!

—Carol Tetzlaff, speaker, author, *Ezra: Unleashing the Power of Praise, Restoring Broken to Beautiful through Worship*

A mom. Her son. And the almighty God who created them both. This book nails every mother who has ever taken a deep breath and prayed for the impossible through gritted teeth, hot tears, and raw emotion. When tragedy hit the Custodio home, Christina braced for the bad news, but she never gave up hope that God could perform a miracle. Even in the ever-increasing cliques of those who deny God, there is no denying His eye was on the sparrow, and His hand held the hearts of all who were holding onto hope. The POWER of prayer is nothing short of amazing, and this story proves it!

—Tammy Whitehurst, speaker, author, and co-director
of the Christian Communicators Conference

When the worst happens, where is God? In God Changed His Mind, Christina invites you into the presence and purposes of God when the road feels long and the path dark. This true story provides tangible hope when a mother's heart breaks, and she seeks answers from God. If you could use a dose of hope today, this book is a must read!

—Erica Wiggenhorn, author of *Letting God Be Enough: Why Striving Keeps You Stuck and How Surrender Sets You Free*

WHEN GOD CHANGED
HIS MIND

WHEN GOD CHANGED
HIS MIND

A True Story of Trial, Triumph, and Finding Joy Beyond Circumstances

CHRISTINA CUSTODIO

REDEMPTION
PRESS

Published by Redemption Press, PO Box 427, Enumclaw, WA 98022.
Toll-Free (844) 2REDEEM (273-3336)

Redemption Press is honored to present this title in partnership with the author. The views expressed or implied in this work are those of the author. Redemption Press provides our imprint seal representing design excellence, creative content, and high-quality production.

The author has tried to recreate events, locales, and conversations from memories of them. In order to maintain their anonymity, in some instances the names of individuals, some identifying characteristics, and some details may have been changed, such as physical properties, occupations, and places of residence.

ISBN 13: 978-1-64645-331-3 (Paperback)
978-1-64645-329-0 (ePub)
978-1-64645-330-6 (Mobi)

Library of Congress Catalog Card Number: 2021922963

Isaiah,

There was a time I thought if I had an occasion to make a public statement about you, it would be about who you were. Thank God I've been given the gift to talk about who you are. You are mostly what any mother would hope for her son to be. I say mostly because you often inspire the occasional throat punch. You are everything God intended you to be. Your corny sense of humor, sensitive and thoughtful spirit, and blinding inner light—often revealed in your smile—inspires anyone who knows you to be a better human. You believe you can do anything. Though your confidence repeatedly stresses me out, it also makes me feel great admiration for who you are. Thank you for teaching and leading the rest of us to live out a joy-filled life. Thank you for remaining unapologetically you.

I love you, son.

CONTENTS

FOREWORD

In October of 2017, I had the opportunity to meet Christina. We sat across the table from each other and talked about our shared interest in writing and ministry. As our conversation continued, she shared the story of nearly losing her son, Isaiah, to a sudden life-threatening brain bleed, just two years prior at football practice.

As I sat listening, I was pierced to the heart. I could see right away that her determination and belief in God didn't allow her to settle for being a bystander to the situation she faced. Instead, she moved forward with clear vision. She was like a lioness, motivated by fierce love for her son. When some people may have surrendered to the worst and thrown up their hands, she continued to move forward in faith. She refused to accept the hopeless possibilities and instead leaned fully into the God of the impossible.

This same faith that is so evident in Christina, I also saw when I met Isaiah. I could see great peace, assurance, and confidence in him. He is an effective communicator and radiates a contagious joy. You can tell his parents have fought the hard battle for his life through the blood, sweat, and tears of prayer. I wouldn't have believed the incredible, yet difficult journey he had been on if I had not heard it. He is evidence that God is still working miracles.

As a lover of stories and a storyteller myself, I continue to be drawn in by this story as I see the way the Lord has weaved his sovereignty into the fabric of the lives of the Custodio family. Christina shares not only the mountain top experiences but the valleys as well. She reveals God's presence in every part of it as she invites us to walk along the path of a mother, sometimes feeling lost, but trusting in the Lord to guide each step.

If you are fighting a battle of your own or for your child, and the odds seem stacked up against you, I know you will be inspired and encouraged by Christina's story to bravely trust God through every circumstance. We all have trials and tribulations in this world, and there are many escape routes that we can take to run from our pain. We can give up, detach from life, turn to addiction, the affection of others, anger, or bitterness. Through this story of hope, you will be inspired to continue persevering. No matter what things look like before you, behind you, on either side of you, you will be able to find a message that speaks directly to your situation through the words of this book.

During a time of great tribulation in our world and always, we need God. He is the pipeline of life, hope, healing, and breath. Without him, nothing exists so we must go to the source for all our needs. As you read, you will see how Christina and her family chose the Source of Life in their darkest hour, and you can too.

—Karen Abercrombie, actress (*The War Room*), producer (*Discarded Things*), writer

ACKNOWLEDGMENTS

I must first thank my husband, Ozzy, who is and always has been my biggest cheerleader—even when I've rolled my eyes at him after he told me I'm amazing and can do anything. Thank you. I love you.

Thanks to my mom and dad, Ed and Catherine Nunnely, who, even though I'm a grown woman, tell me they are proud of me. Thank you for your encouragement and love.

My girls, Abrianna and Olivia, are always willing to listen to and support my antics and speak truth when they tell me I'm funnier than their dad.

Dr. Christopher Troup, you are our hero. Thank you for being the heart and hands of the great Healer. You mean so much to us.

Thank you to the ICU staff and the Roger C. Peace teams (inpatient and outpatient) for helping to keep Isaiah not only alive but also able to thrive.

My sister-friend Jamie has been the most loyal, authentic, and encouraging-in-every-way friend I could ever ask for. I'm grateful for you.

My Holland Park Church family for the love and support they provided that night especially.

Thank you to my Christian Communicator Conference sisters who were key in kicking me off on this speaking and writing path I'm on.

Big thanks to Athena Dean Holtz and my Redemption Press family who have truly become family. Thank you for supporting and helping me be the best version of myself.

Thank you, Jason Ayers, for your care and expertise visually documenting parts of our story. We're ready for the movie!

Thank you to the thousands of online friends who have loved us, encouraged us, and supported us for so many years. You are part of the reason we are here.

For their financial sacrifice, I owe a great deal of gratitude to Dale and Beverly McCorkle, Steven and Sarah DeLisle, and Kirsten Zinkann and the Keller Williams Greenville Central family. You made the difference.

PART 1

A BOY ON LOAN

CHAPTER 1

GOD COMES FOR ISAIAH

From the time he was born, I always knew my son, Isaiah, would die young. This knowing always lingered in the back of my mind. Nothing about him justified my expectation. I just knew. So when the day finally arrived, I wasn't shocked.

Football practice started at six o'clock every weekday evening. It was Tuesday, and I drove Isaiah to the middle school field as usual on that scorching hot September day typical of South Carolina. On our way, we talked about how psyched he was to play in the first D Team game of the season. The D Team is the first level of high school football and starts in the eighth grade, so we were all anticipating this new experience. Isaiah told me that since they would play on the day his *abuelita* (grandmother) had died three years previously, he would dedicate the game to her.

We stopped at a traffic light, and I said, "Isaiah, let me take a picture to commemorate this moment."

"Wait," he said, reaching down to snag the helmet resting between his feet. "I want my helmet in the picture." He sat back and put on his game face. He refused to look at the camera and smile, though, because he wanted to look tough.

I'll take what I can get. I centered him on the screen and captured the picture as the traffic light turned green. It turned out really cool. I smiled the rest of the drive, thinking about how—similar to my two girls—he usually argued about pictures, leaving me with a whole library of blurred, hand-covering-his-face photos on my phone.

I stopped in front of the field entrance. Isaiah opened the door and leaped out of my husband Ozzy's ugly light-green Ford sedan I was driving before I could even put it in park. As he sprinted onto the field, I yelled, "Have fun. Be safe!"

From there, I headed to the store to do some grocery shopping, then home. I was a long-term substitute teacher at the middle school and had already worked a full day with the English for Speakers of Other Languages (ESOL) class. I was ready to be home and done. But as I put the groceries away, I heard my phone ring and answered it. It was the trainer at the middle school. Isaiah had a bad headache, and the trainer asked me to pick him up. I figured it was only a headache, and he'd be okay for a few more minutes, so I continued putting the groceries away.

But then a thought arose—*I shouldn't make him suffer with head pain*—and a feeling came over me that I should go right away. I yelled out to the girls, who were doing their homework upstairs, that I would be right back, jumped into the car, pulled out of the driveway, and headed toward the school. It would be my third trip to the middle school that day. I couldn't believe I had to go back.

As I drove down our street, I remembered that I had forgotten to call back my friend Page, so I dialed her number to finish telling her a story I had started earlier in the day. When I arrived at the field, I sat in the car to finish my conversation. I figured Isaiah would see me and walk over. I continued talking but watched as the trainer and one of the coaches picked him up off the ground. They were on either side of him, and his legs were dragging. "Oh my goodness, Page, this boy is so dramatic. Let me get off this phone and see what's going on. I'll call you back."

I stepped out of the car and dropped my mom voice on him. "Isaiah." He didn't look up. I quickly realized this was no performance. He was sick and incoherent. He couldn't even walk on his own. Together, the coach and trainer sat him down on a water cooler. That's when he started to vomit. We tried to get him to drink some water, but it poured out of his mouth.

He tried to speak but couldn't get out a complete sentence. His words were slow and slurred as he forced out, "Home. Home. Hurt. Home. Hurt." Then he looked up at me through glassy and desperate eyes and said, "Help."

His last word took my breath away. Something was wrong. "Maybe we should go to the hospital." We struggled to get him into the back seat of the car. He had little control of his own body, so we laid him back there with no seatbelt. He was unable to sit up, and I didn't have time to worry about it. I called Ozzy at work, but he didn't answer, so I left him a message telling him what was happening. I called my parents' house next, and my dad answered. My parents lived right around the corner from the school. I explained what was happening, that I couldn't reach Ozzy, and that I might take Isaiah to the hospital. My dad said he would meet me at the school and that he would bring water and try to see what was wrong.

After the call ended, that uneasy feeling grew, so I decided I didn't want to wait before going to the hospital. As I drove down the long driveway of the middle school, I called Ozzy again and told him to meet us at the emergency room. I then called my dad again and told him of my plans. He had already left home and wasn't far from us. He would follow us to the ER.

As we drove down the street, nearing the highway entrance, Isaiah rolled onto the floor.

"Isaiah. Isaiah! Get up, son. Isaiah! You have to get up. Get off the floor! I can't stop!"

I reached one hand behind me and shook him the best I could while driving. My heart pounded, and my body trembled. *What could be so wrong that he can't control his body?* I now realize angels must have been in the car with us because he was somehow back up on the seat when I turned around again. I pulled over into a parking lot, then called my dad again. I told him I had stopped and to please come and give me some of that water. He pulled into the parking lot only a minute behind me. We tried once again to get Isaiah to drink water, but he wasn't responding. I had to get back on the road and to the hospital.

We made it to the hospital emergency entrance, where my dad pulled up in his big white SUV right behind me. He jumped out, ran in through the emergency room doors, and found a man in scrubs who could bring out a wheelchair. Somehow Isaiah helped get himself into the chair, and that's where his responsiveness ended. The attendant immediately took him back to a room and put him in a bed while I nervously filled out paperwork with our insurance information. I knew something was wrong, but I figured he was severely dehydrated or something. Ozzy had arrived by then, and when I finished the forms, he and my dad joined me in the room with Isaiah.

Nurse Bob was in the room and introduced himself, letting us know he would be taking care of Isaiah. He hooked him up to some monitors, then left the room. More time passed than I was comfortable with before anyone did anything for him. He was lying there with glassy eyes, not responding to anything we said. He would often move an arm or a leg, but nothing about it looked voluntary.

I decided to take matters into my own hands. I'm not a doctor, but sometimes I pretend to be in my spare time. Something inside me told me to look into his eyes. I leaned over, close to his face, and looked deep. I didn't see anything move. *Aren't his pupils supposed to move?* I pulled out my cell phone and turned on the flashlight. I shined the light into his eyes for a better look. Nothing. Then I noticed that one pupil was larger than the other. *That's not right.*

"Something is really wrong. Get the nurse."

Ozzy went to get help while my dad positioned his phone to take a picture. I glanced at him, feeling irritated with his timing.

Nurse Bob came back promptly, looked into Isaiah's eyes, and then immediately left the room. My stomach turned. *It's bad.* Bob came back with another person to help him transport Isaiah to radiology to get a CT scan. After they left the room, I looked at Ozzy and my dad. I was shaking. "I think it's his brain. Something is wrong with his brain."

My dad raised an eyebrow and frowned. "Christina, you're not a doctor. Don't go making up stuff you don't know about."

I shook my head and said quietly, "I just have a feeling."

When they brought Isaiah back from the scan, I searched Bob's face for a report. "Bob, it's serious, isn't it?"

"Yes, it is."

I appreciated his honest answer and quick response. "What is it?"

He didn't answer. He kept his focus on Isaiah as he dealt with the various wires monitoring my son's vitals.

"You might as well tell me because if you don't, I'm just gonna google it," I threatened.

He turned and walked over to me and looked directly in my face. "Do not google it. As a parent, I am telling you, do not google it."

I knew then the problem was more serious than I could imagine, but Bob was calm, so I was too. It wasn't long before an ER doctor came in to give us the news. Isaiah had a severe brain hemorrhage, and his brain was filling up with blood. Though I had felt it was serious, the report still shocked me. My spirit may have left my body for a moment. The doctor continued explaining, telling us Isaiah would be airlifted to Greenville Memorial Children's Hospital. There, a pediatric neurosurgeon would perform emergency surgery, cutting into my baby's skull with the intent of saving his life.

I felt as if my body might start to convulse. *This is it. I can't believe this. How is this happening right now?* I frantically sent out SOS texts to various friends, asking for prayer.

Nurse Bob continued to give us more information as he received it. He acted quickly and kept his composure. Before long, he told us it was time for Ozzy, my dad, and me to go to the Children's Hospital, where we would meet Isaiah and his medical team. We walked out of the room, but as I moved farther from the door and the sounds of the machines beeping and swishing began to fade, my anxiety grew. We walked down the hall a few yards, then I turned around, wanting to run back into the room and hold my baby boy again in case it was the last time. As soon as I turned, I saw Bob standing in the doorway watching me.

It clearly wasn't his first mom rodeo. He caught my eye and mouthed, *It's okay. Go.*

I nodded, then turned back and took a few more steps down the hall. I couldn't help it. I turned around again.

Again, Bob's eyes met mine. "It's okay, Mom," he said.

Okay. I turned back around, set my focus on the exit, and headed out.

The gospel writer Luke mentions that in one of Jesus's lowest and most difficult moments, in the garden of Gethsemane, "an angel from heaven appeared and strengthened him" (Luke 22:43 NLT). Though I don't think Bob was literally an angel from heaven, I do believe God placed him in the ER during those couple of hours specifically for my family and me. God works through regular people. Sometimes we search for a grand show of His presence when He has already placed a friend, a stranger, a nurse, a doctor, a custodian, a child—anyone who can speak to us in some way—to do His work.

With Ozzy right behind me, my shaking legs carried me outside to the now-darkened sky and my even darker SUV Ozzy had been driving. Ozzy and I couldn't even speak. *How had all this happened?* As I opened the car door, I heard someone yell my name, so I turned around.

Through the darkness and glare of the hospital lights, all I could see was my brother-in-law Eddie running toward me with a nurse by his side. *When did he arrive?* The nurse was crying. *Oh my God, please no. No.* I knew they were coming to tell me that my only son had died before he could make his flight.

CHAPTER 2

LOST

As my eyes adjusted to the darkness and the nurse's face came into focus, I realized she wasn't just any nurse—she was my friend LeAnne, who worked in the ER. Tears streamed down her face as she grabbed me in a tight embrace. She then turned my body toward the ambulance bay. "The helicopter didn't come. They went to the wrong hospital. Go to the ambulance and be with your baby!"

I headed in the direction she turned my body and eventually made it to the ambulance. I tried to climb in the back with Isaiah, but an EMT stopped me and directed me to the front of the ambulance. I trembled as I climbed in next to the driver. He did his best to make small talk, but I didn't want to talk to him. I kept turning around to look in the back of the ambulance to see if my boy was still alive. I watched as the other EMT with him cut off his clothes. *Please don't die. Please don't die. Don't die in this ambulance. God, don't let him die. Please let us make it to the hospital.*

We made it to the hospital, and I stepped out of the passenger seat into my own personal fog. Someone escorted me to the waiting room, where I felt more alone than I ever had in my life. I knew Ozzy, my dad, and my brother-in-law were not far behind, but they couldn't get there fast enough.

After I entered the room, I stopped and looked around. I couldn't figure out where to place my next step. I couldn't find the logic behind the room in which I was standing. Apparently, I looked lost because a woman there with her family asked me why I had come. I found a chair and sat down. Somehow I choked out a vague description of what was happening.

The woman tilted her head in a solemn and gentle nod. Her eyes grew wide and shiny, her eyebrows raised. She was like a light in the fog. "Can I pray with you?"

I could barely get the word out of my mouth. "Yes."

She walked over, grabbed my hands, knelt in front of me, and began to pray for Isaiah and me. I sobbed quietly as she prayed. When she finished, I thanked her and asked why she was there. Her son, who was much younger than Isaiah, was in surgery but was, as far as I understood, in much worse condition than Isaiah. Almost every organ in his body was shutting down. His medical condition was something they had been dealing with for years. This woman was possibly moments from losing her son, yet she knelt down on her knees for mine. That was a love I had never experienced before from a stranger.

It wasn't long before my guys walked into the room, and not too far behind them, more family and church friends began pouring in. One by one, they filled the room—my friend Amy; our pastor, Matt; my sister-in-law Sandee (Eddie's wife). Red and watery eyes, stifled sniffles, nervous smiles—that's how our friends appeared, but it was a beautiful sight. The family that had been there before I arrived quietly moved to another room to make space for our growing group. First there were about fifteen, then twenty, and then still more came.

I was mostly okay until my friend Sarah hugged me. Then I broke down. "I can't believe this. What is happening?" I took a deep breath to dry it up and get back to my primary responsibility and habit of greeting everyone and ensuring they had a place to sit.

For such a scary time, we kept the mood light. I did my best to smile and joke with everyone until I glanced over at Ozzy, sitting on the couch next to me. Tears streamed down his face. He was losing it. He couldn't even fake it. He mumbled, "Why is this happening? Why can't it be me? Why?"

I wish I could say I immediately wrapped my arms around him to give him comfort, but I didn't. I felt angry. *Why can't you keep it together! He's not dead! Stop acting like he is!* That's what I screamed inside my head, but I knew better than to say it out loud. I moved closer to him so we were touching, then turned my attention to a random conversation elsewhere in the room.

At some point, a woman in scrubs came into the room and stood in front of me. It felt as though she were shoving papers and a pen in my face, telling me to sign all control away. Something about allowing them to cut into my son. Something about not holding them responsible if he died, blah, blah, blah. I wanted to scream, *Are you kidding me? My son is dying, and you're putting this in my face! Can't someone else do this? I'm his mother! Why would you do this to me?* I was trembling so badly, I'm sure my name was illegible, but I did manage to scribble something on the signature line, as well as suppress my inclination to scream. Every so often, I would look up and see more friends in the room, many I hadn't even noticed enter.

People continued to come over the next hour. My friend Philip had picked up my mom (Nani) and my two girls, Abrianna, fourteen, and Olivia, ten, from the house. Our pastor's wife, Ashley, had found an emergency babysitter to watch their kids and joined her husband, Matt, to be with us at the hospital. So many were there to support us. So many made sacrifices to be there.

When Dr. Gwyn, the head of pediatric surgery, walked in and saw more than thirty heads turn to hear his news, he asked if he could speak to Ozzy and me privately. We told him they were all friends we considered family, and he could speak freely. He was a tall, dark-skinned, kind-looking man. He wore a long knit sweater with his name embroidered on it in the corner. Later, we found out his wife had crocheted it for him because it was softer than a typical doctor's coat. He wore it proudly. He sat down in the middle of the floor and told us who Isaiah's surgeon would be and what the medical team would try to do for Isaiah. He let us know the surgeon would be in later to talk to us. We thanked him, and he walked back to check on the team with Isaiah.

About twenty minutes later, another doctor walked into the room. He introduced himself as Dr. Christopher Troup. He didn't look like a brain surgeon, and he didn't sound like one, but he was indeed the surgeon. Someone pulled a chair into the middle of the room and offered it to him. He sat down and explained that Isaiah's brain was filling up with blood, and the organs in his body were shutting down. He let us know what he planned to do and proceeded to tell us in two or three different ways that Isaiah could die on the table. He was tender but direct. He would do everything he could, but we needed to understand the potential for death.

He was still talking when I interrupted. "Excuse me. I don't know if you are legally required to continue talking, but I got it. I understand. Can you please go fix him now?"

"Yes, ma'am," he responded gently, then proceeded to exit the room as several of us thanked him.

The collective emotion in the room was heavy, but we finally knew exactly what we were dealing with. I looked at my girls sitting next to each other on a couch covered with tacky upholstery. Olivia, the youngest, seemed fine. She was playing with a handheld video game. I don't think she understood the magnitude of the situation. Abrianna was hardly moving. I asked her if she was okay.

She responded with little emotion. "Yes."

"Do you want to talk about it?"

"No, I'm fine."

Abrianna is not one to give in to or show her emotions in public. I knew she needed more attention or comfort, but I wasn't going to force her to talk in front of all those people.

I learned later that, hours before, as she was waiting for Philip to pick her and Olivia up from home and bring them to the hospital, she had held a conversation with God. Based on my tone when I talked to her on the phone, she instinctively knew that Isaiah's condition was life-threatening. Abrianna was only fourteen years old, at the start of ninth grade, and was trying to figure out where to place those emotions. All she could think to do was set her unfinished business straight. She remembered that she owed us twenty dollars for something. So she grabbed the cash from her room, walked into our bedroom, raised it to the sky, and pleaded.

"Look, God! I'm paying them back! Now, please let him be okay!" She set the money on our ironing board like a lamb on an altar, then went downstairs to wait for her ride.

If you had asked me before that night how I would handle losing one of my children, I would have told you I could never survive it. I would have begged for the mercy of my own death. I always believed God would take my son young, but I never said I could endure it. That night, when Isaiah's death stared me mockingly in the face, I tried to escape it. I stood up from the scratchy, tear-stained couch of the waiting room where so many friends and family were surrounding Ozzy and me with love and prayers and walked through the fog into the bathroom.

I wasn't crying. I wasn't hysterical. I was scared. I shut the door behind me, then allowed the tears to stream down my face. My legs were shaking so badly I could hardly stand.

I whispered defiantly, "God, he's only thirteen. Seriously? You're going to take him now?" I remembered seeing Scriptures that talked about God changing His mind (whatever that meant), so I begged Him over and over to change His mind. "Change your mind, change your mind, change your mind, change your mind, change your mind." That's all I could think of to say to Him, so I said it over and over again. If there had been a clean corner, I would have been sitting in it rocking. Tears streamed down my face, and my body shook with a fear I had never before experienced.

I dried my face, took a deep breath, then walked out of the bathroom. The atmosphere was tense, but everyone continued to do their best to keep up the small talk. I had to keep my emotions together. If I lost it, then everyone else would too, and I couldn't do that to them. I headed toward the couch and began planning my son's funeral, how I would tell his sisters, how I would survive, and wondering if my marriage could take this kind of blow. Although I was afraid of dealing with that kind of reality, I still had some sort of crazy peace. It was mind-blowing, but I knew if God decided to take him, I would survive it. I would be okay, and I could even thrive despite it. It was a miraculous feeling and reaction to a scenario I never imagined stepping into with any kind of peace or grace. But there it was, staring me in my face, and I knew I would be okay.

Still, I begged for my son's life. What no one in the room knew other than me, Ozzy, Eddie, and Sandee was that midnight, September 9, was the third anniversary of my beautiful mother-in-law's death after battling cancer for many years. We were all thinking but would not say out loud that we couldn't handle losing our Isaiah on the same day. The surgeon began cutting into his skull at 11:12 p.m. on September 8. Ozzy later confessed he watched the clock the whole time. I remember having a moment of anxiety once the clock struck midnight. I could picture Ozzy's mom waiting at the gates to take Isaiah's hand and lead him home.

I knew God was going to take him. I wasn't pessimistic. I wasn't overly dramatic. I wasn't a crazy, emotional mother. I just knew it. I've always been very aware my children are on loan. From day one, I dedicated them to God, knowing they were truly His. Though it sounds strange, I knew God was going to take Isaiah from me. So when we learned the severity of what was happening, I knew the day I always feared had come.

CHAPTER 3

A MULTITUDE OF PRAYERS

As I sat, I could sense the glances of my friends and family. They were wondering if I were okay. They were waiting for a breakdown. No one seemed to know what to say about the heaviness of the situation. I could smell the fried chicken that someone had brought earlier. I glanced over at the table against the wall. Random bags and boxes of fast food sat there, waiting for consumption. It was like a church potluck, except no one had time to make their best potluck dish. Various conversations and prayers floated through the air like the calming sound of crashing waves you hear but aren't entirely conscious of. Anything was better than discussing my son's impending death beneath the heavy emotional cloud hovering over the room. I was dying to be with Isaiah, but upon our request, a nurse had denied us access to him. She told us there wasn't time.

Our pastor, Matt, asked us to join hands as he prayed. He spoke for each of us when he promised that if God chose to save Isaiah's life, we would honor and glorify Him through it. Together we committed to sharing the story of redemption we believed our Creator was writing. A few others petitioned God out loud, and then we ended our petitions with amens. I opened my eyes and looked up to see my friend Michelle grinning at me.

"I think he's going to be okay," she said. "Yeah, I feel good about it."

Her grin was contagious, and I grinned back. "Yeah? Okay. I believe you."

After that time of prayer, I felt calmer. We had presented our precious boy to the Creator. We placed Isaiah in the Lord's hands and left him there.

Not much later, we heard what we knew to be the sound of a bed on wheels coming near the door. Several medical personnel pushed a patient down the hall. My friend Amy, who had been diligent since she arrived about catching and communicating any information I might miss, jumped up. "Christina, Ozzy. I think that's Isaiah. Go. Go now!"

I looked at her, uncertain I dared to defy an earlier command to stay put. But there wasn't time to think.

"Go."

I jumped up and sprinted toward the sound of a squeaky wheel. I saw Isaiah on the bed. "Ozzy, let's go!" He was still in a lamenting daze. We identified ourselves as the patient's parents and asked if we could go with them. They said we could, but we had to put on scrubs and masks before entering the operating room area. We quickly and clumsily put the blue paper clothes over our own and entered the elevator, joining the medical caravan.

I leaned over and whispered into my dying boy's ear. "Isaiah, it's Mom. We are here. Your dad and I are here with you. You are okay. We love you so much. I love you, baby."

Tears streamed down Ozzy's face. We reached our destination floor and stepped out. We walked a little way, then stopped in front of Isaiah's operating room. There, Dr. Troup introduced his whole medical team: nurses, anesthesiologists, another surgeon, and other random people. I could barely see them through my burning, watery eyes.

"Do you have any questions before we take him in?" Dr. Troup asked.

Of course, I had questions. *How good of a surgeon are you? How long will it take? Will he live? Do you promise you won't mess up? Why is this happening?* All I could get out was, "Do you pray?"

"Yes, ma'am, I do." Then, as if a magical spell had come over each of them, they formed a circle around Isaiah. Ozzy and I stood there holding hands as Dr. Troup began to pray over our baby. I cried as

I listened to him petition the One he knew was in control. He knew the Great Physician. He knew if anyone were going to save Isaiah's life, it would be the One who created him. The Great Physician would work through Dr. Troup's well-trained hands.

After we each agreed with the final amen, it was time for them to go. Ozzy and I kissed Isaiah, not knowing if it would be the last time, then watched as the medical team entered what we considered to be the battlefield—where they would use medical weapons to fight for our son's life. Ozzy and I stood there alone outside of the room, not knowing what to do. I looked up at him. "Are you okay now? 'Cause you were . . ." I took a deep breath. "Never mind."

"Yes, I'm good. That was awesome."

"Yeah, it really was," I answered.

He took my hand, and we headed back to the elevator and back to our own team of friends and family. We continued our time of fellowship while we waited. People continued to bring food through-out the night, as a good church family knows how to do. We invited others who were waiting for their loved ones to emerge from surgeries, comas, or whatever life-threatening reason they were in that place to join in our feast. This would not be a time for mourning. Our boy was still alive.

As promised, after the first hour of surgery, a nurse from the operating room called my cell phone, letting me know everything was going as well as could be expected. Isaiah was stable, and Dr. Troup was still working on him. She asked if there was anything I needed.

"No, just prayer."

"Okay," she answered, and then she prayed right there on the phone. Once again, prayer induced tears.

When she finished, I choked out, "Thank you."

I looked up, and I saw everyone staring at me. "Everything is good. He's stable, and that woman just prayed with me over the phone," I said, crying. We all felt more relaxed after the first phone call. Though I trusted God, I still wasn't entirely convinced we would be allowed to keep Isaiah here on earth. Another hour passed, and I received a second phone call. Still stable. Still working. The third hour came, and I was so preoccupied, I missed it. I tried to call back, but no answer. *Breathe, Christina. It's okay. He's okay,* I told myself.

Another hour passed since missing the third phone call. Some of the waiting crew were starting to feel and act a bit loopy. I noticed my friend Sarah looking puzzled at our friend Gina's name tag. Upon arriving at the hospital, our friends had been required to check in, have their picture taken, and wear a printed name tag.

Sarah smirked at Gina and snickered. She had a heavy Southern accent. "Gina! You look like Greg Smith!"

We all looked down at Gina's name tag. Sure enough, her picture looked undeniably like a man from our church. We all howled. We laughed for a good five minutes, tears streaming down some faces. Gina is one of the most put-together friends we have, but she had been ready for bed when she received the text about Isaiah and didn't waste time putting on makeup or a polished outfit.

Gina's "man tag" was the perfect distraction. The clock was ticking. Olivia was asleep and wrapped in a green blanket with a *W* embroidered on its corner that my friend Arlyn Wyatt had brought earlier. About three and a half hours after they began cutting into Isaiah's skull, Dr. Troup appeared in the doorway.

I stopped breathing for a moment. *Say it quick, Doctor.*

"Isaiah is stable."

The room heaved a collective sigh of relief.

Dr. Troup continued to explain how he suctioned mass amounts of blood and blood clots from Isaiah's brain. There was minimal swelling, and they were able to replace the piece of his skull they had cut out.

I couldn't move. I was waiting for the bad news. I didn't feel like celebrating. Isaiah was alive, but what was that life going to look like? Would he know us when he woke up? Would he even wake up? Would he walk or talk? Would we have to take care of him for the rest of our lives?

Ozzy stood up and gave Dr. Troup a great big bear hug, thanking him repeatedly. I smiled and thanked Dr. Troup, but I couldn't move.

I knew God had heard my prayers, *but did He actually change His mind?* Dr. Troup warned us that Isaiah wasn't out of the woods yet, but that stable was good. He left the room, and I felt deep gratitude as I focused on each face in that stale waiting room. Ozzy and I thanked everyone for being there and told them to go home. It was after two in the morning. Some of them decided to stay. They had been there all night and wanted the payoff of seeing Isaiah's living, breathing face.

We continued with hugs and words of thanks as we said good-bye to our prayer soldier friends. We sat and talked with those who remained until a nurse told us that Isaiah was in a room down the hall.

Ozzy and I headed back toward Isaiah's pediatric intensive care unit (PICU) room. I was doing my best to breathe with every step that brought me closer to him. A nurse met us in the hallway and introduced herself as Clarissa. She was kind and gentle. She explained that she would be taking care of Isaiah and that if we needed anything, she would be glad to help as much as she could.

She also let us know that as Isaiah was coming out of surgery, he was fighting off the tubes and monitors. He was pushing everything and everyone he could out of his way. That was a good sign, and the medical staff marveled at his strength. For his protection, however, they had needed to put him in an induced coma. That state would ensure he remained calm, and it would protect his vitals.

I braced myself, prepared to see something like Frankenstein's monster lying in a hospital bed. He looked better than I imagined he would. His head was bandaged heavily on the left side. His face looked swollen, but it was beautiful. He looked so peaceful lying there.

About ten or fifteen minutes after we entered the room, our pastor, Matt, came in. He didn't say anything or look at either one of us. He immediately knelt at the end of Isaiah's bed and prayed. I don't know what he said, but I'm sure it was a prayer of thanksgiving and praise. Ozzy and I both held back tears, continuing our prayers of thanksgiving and praise as well.

I knew we needed to get some sleep, but I didn't want to take my eyes off Isaiah. My fears and emotions felt similar to when he was a newborn. I was exhausted but too afraid he would die if I didn't always keep one eye open and on him. *What if he stops breathing? What if he dies while my eyes are closed?* As if my eyeballs had life-sustaining power. I said a prayer, then cuddled up with Ozzy on the chair that lay flat to make a bed. We had no option but to lie in a way that allowed us to fit together in puzzle formation to somehow escape a fall to the floor.

We lay there and possibly slept for twenty to thirty minutes. When we opened our eyes, shortly after three in the morning, we looked out the glass walls and saw our friend Geoff from church coming down the hall. He had stopped by on his way to work as a local news anchor. He was visibly emotional as his eyes fell upon Isaiah lying in the bed. As he prayed over him, Ozzy and I left the room and gave him some time with Isaiah.

We found out later that when Geoff had woken up that morning and found out what was happening with Isaiah, he immediately went to social media and called on his followers, asking for prayers. We were so moved to find that over twenty-six hundred people commented, committing to pray, and over four thousand people shared his post asking others to pray.

We believed then that those prayers made a difference in the kingdom. We believed they made a difference, but how big we didn't know. The doctors still couldn't tell us anything about what Isaiah's life would look like when he woke up—if he woke up.

We lay back down on our chair-bed. I listened to the swishing of the ventilator that worked for Isaiah's lungs. I heard the beeping of several alarms of the numerous machines monitoring the various functions of his body. If I closed my eyes, I could almost hear a song within the rhythmic noise. I wondered if we would have to choose music for his funeral, or would we get to celebrate his high school graduation, his wedding, or even his next birthday? Until I knew what our chances were for the future, I could not celebrate.

CHAPTER 4

ON WATCH

Tuesday night melted into Wednesday morning. After lying on the chair-bed for a little while, pretending to be asleep while medical personnel came in and out of the room, we gave up and decided to sit up and stare at Isaiah. It was still only six o'clock, so we knew we had a long day ahead of us.

As daylight broke through the slats of the blinds, friends found their way through the halls of the hospital to visit. They weren't used to seeing Isaiah lying unconscious in a hospital bed, and it was difficult for some of the younger ones to see him that way. It seemed most difficult for his older sister, Abrianna. She was strong though visibly shaken when she saw her brother unconscious. Her eyes welled up with tears, but she refused to let them fall.

Our youngest daughter, Olivia, didn't seem to understand what was happening. She was quiet and respectful of the gravity of the situation though she didn't carry the weight of it herself. She was ten years old and had no true concept of death or even potential death. I did not want to set that burden on her. She will know it one day.

We continued to have visitors throughout the day, most of whom would ask me if I had eaten or slept, expressing their importance. I was well aware I needed to eat. I knew I needed to sleep, but I felt if one more person tried to tell me what to do, they might find themselves guests of the hospital we were in. I couldn't eat or sleep—it would distract me from watching Isaiah's every breath.

The day was mostly uneventful. Isaiah remained stable. I found it hard to watch a machine breathe for him, but I was thankful it did. Later that evening, the medical team did a CT scan of his brain. It showed improvement! The remaining blood looked to be absorbing back into his body. They also spent about an hour and a half trying to wake him up to make sure he could wake up. Then they sedated him again. All seemed to be going as well as could be expected.

The world continued without us. The sun set, and Isaiah rested peacefully, but I could not sleep. Sharing a smaller-than twin-sized bed with your six-foot-three, two-hundred-plus-pound husband is nothing nice. It didn't matter. I was still on life watch. That peace could end at any moment, and every moment felt like a bad dream. I could hardly fathom this was my life. I was sleep deprived, I was dirty, and I hadn't brushed my teeth or changed my clothes in almost forty-eight hours, but I couldn't bring myself to leave that room. It was my baby in that bed.

We didn't even know if he could breathe on his own. I needed to watch every rise and fall of his chest. I needed to watch everything his nurses did so I could do it too. They planned to see if he could breathe on his own the next day. Throughout the night, they reduced the amount of breathing help the ventilator gave him. They were weaning him off it. I prayed all night. *Please, God, let him breathe.*

The next day was Thursday. I was surviving through an unhealthy dose of adrenaline. I had barely slept and hadn't eaten, and that was fine with me. I was on watch. Every moment that passed filled me with gratitude. I found myself whispering to God throughout the day, "Thank you." Visitors continued to come, sharing the same words of gratitude for Isaiah's life. Though they knew he was still asleep, it seemed they all wanted to lay their own eyes on his breathing body. Isaiah had a good night, and he was breathing more and more on his own with each passing hour.

Faster than the medical team ever could have predicted, Isaiah's own breaths began taking over from the respirators, so they continued to wean him off. The progress had been looking good all day. He was still sedated, so they would have to wake him to take him completely off. That was going to be rough. Imagine being a thirteen-year-old boy, waking up with a tube down your throat, unable to take normal breaths. Imagining the panic he would experience when he woke up to that, my anxiety rose.

Eventually, the time came to wake him. I braced myself to endure my own emotional pain of watching the respiratory nurse torturing my son when she pulled the tube out.

His eyes held confusion and fear as they blinked open. He gagged as the tube slithered out from his lungs and through his throat, but hallelujah, the tube was out, and he was breathing on his own. He was still heavily under the influence of the drugs meant to keep him asleep, but he was awake. He peeked out from behind one barely open eye, then closed it again.

I clapped my hands. I could hardly contain myself. "Isaiah, are you awake?"

He slowly opened the one eye again. He heard me. I held back the tears. I knew he was alive, but he was *really* alive!

Within seconds, a million and one questions raced through my mind. Did he know us? Would he be able to speak? Why was there no expression on his face? It didn't matter. I had to focus on the fact that he was alive. I planted kisses all over his face. No response—just another peek from that eye. *That's okay—he needs time.* Ozzy and I looked at each other and smiled. Ozzy is from the Bronx, New York, and in true Bronx style, he would have liked to start break dancing in celebration. But he remained respectful of the place we were in.

Isaiah drifted in and out of sleep throughout the day, though we did our best to keep him awake. It was essential to begin evaluating what kind of brain activity he had. Several times he took his left hand and tried to pry his closed eye open. It was swollen shut, which seemed to aggravate him. The nurses continued to monitor his vitals. His heartbeat was irregular, but Clarissa told us this was a common occurrence in these situations. Common or not, it gave me something else to worry about. I then focused on the sound of the heart-monitoring machine and watched the numbers displaying his heart function. I interrogated more than one nurse, making sure the numbers were what they needed to be in order to sustain life. There was also the feeding tube to think about. Was it clean? Is that how he would eat for the rest of his life? He was a big boy. How could he live like that?

But the next day, a Friday, I had something else to be thankful for. It was Ozzy and my sixteenth wedding anniversary. I was grateful on this day that I was not burying my son. I was grateful on this day that my marriage was intact. We celebrated by taking a walk to the first-floor food court, where our friend Sarah treated us to soup and breadsticks from Au Bon Pain. It was the farthest I had been from Isaiah since he came out of surgery. It was difficult to leave him, but it was our anniversary, so I decided to give Ozzy the gift of my presence—for about twenty minutes.

We soon headed back to the fifth floor. We spent the rest of Friday welcoming visitors and watching Isaiah. The medical staff continued to perform tests, wheeling him in and out of the room as they monitored the blood in his brain. It seemed to be reabsorbing well.

Later that evening, Dr. Troup made an appearance. He gave us more information about what had happened. Though they still were not sure what caused the bleeding, they did know the majority of it was found on the left side of his brain—specifically, the language part. Because it was engulfed in blood, that part had been deprived of oxygen, killing the brain tissue. That pronouncement scared me. Language is made up of words, and words are what we need to communicate, and I feared Isaiah might never speak again. Only time would tell.

We tried to make sure he was comfortable and rested. He continued to sleep most of the time, like a newborn. When he was awake, we didn't see much evidence that he knew what was going on. He wasn't speaking. He was just there. I fought the worry continuing to creep up toward the front of my mind. I needed to focus on the daily victories without peering too far ahead to a potentially dismal future for my beautiful boy.

Saturday morning was surreal. It's not what Saturday should ever feel like. No sleeping in a comfy bed listening to the birds start their morning rituals. No sound of neighbors mowing their grass or kids running, roller skating, or skateboarding down the street. It was an unwelcome reality. I had hardly slept but still had to entertain the many guests that visited throughout the day. I found myself providing comfort to those who were distraught over the sight of Isaiah in that hospital bed. Friends were kind not to mention how bad I looked. My face was drawn, and my eyes were tired. *One day I might care.*

One issue that upset me was that Isaiah had no facial expressions even though he was awake. His emotions had always radiated from his face, so seeing him lying in that bed expressionless bothered me. I wondered if he would ever regain that part of himself or if this was it. I was grateful, however, that he seemed to be waking up more and more as Saturday went on. Ozzy and I were in the room talking to him as we continued to do each day, asking him yes or no questions, to which he would nod or shake his head. We weren't always sure if he responded with the answer he meant, but we were thankful for a response. This time, as we were talking, it looked as if he smiled a little bit. I almost did a flip, but I wasn't sure if he had intended to smile or if it was a fluke.

"Isaiah! Did you just smile?"

He nodded yes.

I wondered if he could do it again. "Smile at your dad."

He did it again.

Hallelujah! I was full of joy and gratitude. *He's coming back.* My eyes welled up with tears. That was the best part of the day. That was all he gave us that day, but we were grateful.

Sunday ended up being a tough one. He seemed so tired, but I had no idea what he could be thinking or feeling. He mostly seemed to be simply existing. Our friends Belinda and Mia, a mother and daughter, visited that morning. They serenaded Isaiah with a gospel song. Although the rendition was moving, Isaiah wasn't so moved.

He closed his eyes and pretended to go to sleep. I reassured them that they sang beautifully and that Isaiah was simply exhausted.

After they left, it occurred to me that Isaiah might be tired of visitors, so I asked. "Isaiah, are you okay with all of the people coming to visit you?"

He shook his head no.

I felt terrible that I had never considered asking him before that day. Of course, he had seemed unbothered. We couldn't see any expression of emotion. I assumed he would enjoy the company but didn't think about how not being able to speak might have been frustrating for him as he might have felt pressure to say something to his guests. Isaiah had always been an outgoing kid who did his best to make others feel welcome in his presence.

The language part of his brain had essentially died. The only hope for him to speak again was for his brain to make new connections to enable him to do so, ultimately creating a new language center. The only way Isaiah knew how to handle the frustration of this new normal was to close his eyes and "check out."

As we considered all the things that could be wrong, we realized he wasn't moving anything on the right side of his body. How had we not noticed that before? We mentioned it to Dr. Gwyn, who had been coming in at least once every day, but he was not worried about it. He said it was normal and wouldn't last forever. I was counting on it.

Since it was Sunday, we didn't expect any kind of therapist to make an appearance, but Karla, a pediatric physical therapist, came in anyway. She wasn't wasting any time. He couldn't even move one side of his body and hadn't been upright in five days. I wondered what she could possibly do for him.

She was able to get him up on the side of the bed. It was exceedingly difficult, and he looked miserable. He was able to stay up for ten to fifteen minutes before his body appeared pulled by some kind of invisible force back to the safety of his bed. She was proud of him and said the fact he could stay up even that long was remarkable. I guess she didn't expect much when she came in, especially after looking at his chart. The nurses and doctors had all told us Isaiah would take some steps forward and some backward, so that's what Ozzy and I prepared to see.

Isaiah had more miserable moments. He was waking up more and more with every hour that passed and became increasingly agitated. He didn't understand what had happened to him. We kept trying to explain little bits of his story, but he didn't seem to get it. We would explain one detail, then have to explain it again a few hours later.

Monday came with new challenges. Isaiah still had a catheter in, which must be a strange experience for a thirteen-year-old boy. He noticed that something wasn't right in that region of his body and was visibly irritated by it. It was important to change it regularly to keep it clean, so Crystal, the nurse who had relieved Clarissa the day before, came in to change the catheter.

She decided that maybe a condom catheter would work better for him and be more comfortable. Yes, a condom catheter is exactly what it sounds like. She replaced the standard catheter with the new one and asked him how it felt. He reached down with his left hand and tried to pull it off. Thankfully, he had not mastered the use of his left hand yet and was unsuccessful. *Lord, have mercy.* We kept grabbing his hand, telling him he needed to leave it alone and that if he pulled it, he could hurt himself. We continued to reprimand and push his hand away until Crystal decided to take another look at it.

The look on her face shifted from care to distress. "Oh no!"

The catheter had rolled down with some of his hair in it and was pulling, causing him pain. He didn't know how to tell us. Crystal looked at me apologetically and then back at Isaiah. She quickly grabbed some medical scissors and carefully cut the hair in order to remove the catheter with less trauma. It was then she decided he would just have to wear an adult diaper. She refused to subject him to any more pain and suffering.

When she finished cleaning him up and fitting him with the diaper, she leaned down in front of Isaiah's sweet face, looking directly into his eyes. She was close to tears. "Isaiah, I'm so sorry, sweet boy. I'm sorry I hurt you."

That's when it happened. That's when we saw our Isaiah emerge from the depths of the damaged brain he had been trapped in for days. He looked up at Crystal with the most tender eyes and reached for her with his only functioning hand and wrapped his arm around her, bringing her in close for a hug. He could see she was hurting, so he comforted her. At that point, tears flowed from both our eyes. She sat up to dry her face. He then grabbed her hand and held it tight. Our sweet boy was still in there.

I felt warm and cold at the same time. In that same moment, I felt trauma and comfort. It was a juxtaposition of emotions, but at the end of it all was gratitude. Still, I wondered if this would be what the rest of Isaiah's life would look like—glimpses of who he used to be, then back to a boy imprisoned behind walls of dead tissue.

To make matters worse, Ozzy and I realized that the whole time we had been eating our meals in front of him, Isaiah was dying for a bite. He just couldn't verbalize his need. That evening, he reached for the dinner the hospital dining service had delivered for me. The tube carrying his liquid meals through his nose and down into his stomach wasn't cutting it. Forget hunger pains—my heart was hurting for my hungry boy. I worried he would never be able to enjoy the taste of food again.

We continued to keep watch.

CHAPTER 5

THE BOX OF PEACE

Tuesday morning brought new challenges. It seemed Isaiah woke up and realized he was living a life he didn't want and was highly disappointed. He was on the verge of tears. He wanted to eat. He hadn't eaten for an entire six days and tried everything possible to figure out a way to remove his feeding tube. I would have, too, if I were him. Unfortunately, for his safety, they had to put him in restraints. It was difficult to watch. My heart had never been ripped apart so many times within one week.

Although I watched my son experience so much trauma, I couldn't allow it to overcome me. I refused to break down. I decided to put all my fears and emotions in a separate place. I imagined God himself held them in a beautiful box of peace. They were safe there.

The medical staff started calling Isaiah "Houdini." He figured out all kinds of ways to get out of those restraints. Desperation birthed creativity within the moments, hours, and days of his hospital "imprisonment." We never did figure out his methods.

The nurses finally realized they somehow needed to get real food inside our growing boy. The best part of Tuesday came with the introduction of that food. He had two servings of pears, two containers of juice, a little water, and some chocolate cake. Then he had almost a whole banana and a few spoonsfuls of mac 'n' cheese for a snack. Then later—some ice cream. It was a beautiful sight to behold. Crystal explained that they would take his feeding tube out if he continued down that route and ate a good dinner. He nodded to signal that he understood, then I saw a glimmer in his eye I hadn't seen in a while.

Later that day, as Crystal was checking his vitals and such, I was staring at him, as I had been doing for days, and I told him, "I love you."

He nodded his head.

I looked him in the eye. "Isaiah, say, I love you, Mom."

He took a deep breath. "I'm hungry."

At least that's what Crystal and I thought we heard him say. Who cares! I heard his voice. There was praise and celebration. The medical staff continued to be amazed by his progress. I wasn't so amazed. I expected nothing less from my God. To top it all off, they removed his feeding tube. Glory! Just as it is written: Now to him who is able to do immeasurably more than all we ask or imagine, according to his power that is at work within us, to him be glory in the church and in Christ Jesus throughout all generations, for ever and ever! Amen. (Ephesians 3:20–21)

Karla came and pushed Isaiah through physical therapy (PT). He did great. Since he was able to lift and raise his left hand, Isaiah, Crystal, and I decided to do the whip and nae nae dance as part of his therapy. He tried to show me how to do the "stanky legg" properly but had a hard time—just kidding. He couldn't move his legs, but I imagined he did. We tried to keep a good sense of humor through it all.

The next several days would be the most challenging of my life. Ozzy had gone back to work, and the days with Isaiah were exclusively mine and the medical staff's. I did everything for him they would let me do. I helped change his diaper. I helped wipe him down to get clean. I fed him. I kept watch every minute to make sure he was safe. I couldn't bring myself to leave him longer than it took to take a shower down the hall. I hadn't breathed fresh air for an entire seven days. I could barely eat, and I was losing weight. I knew what I looked like based on the expressions of friends who came to visit and were still too kind to say anything. I didn't care. My priority was taking care of my son.

I did my best to keep up with the girls as they navigated our new world without the presence of their mom each day. I was grateful for my parents, who cared for them, ensuring they had everything they needed—except me. It pains me to think of the grief Abrianna and Olivia experienced during that exceedingly difficult road we were all staggering down. I prayed God would cover them—that they would only experience His presence and not the temporary loss of their mother.

Later in the morning, Preston Cole, a college student from church, came by to see Isaiah before going out of town for a golf competition. Isaiah always looked up to Preston. He is a wonderful young man of God. Isaiah had been taking a nap, but when he opened his eyes and saw Preston, his face lit up and he smiled. I'm sure it was a wonderful moment for both of them. I was thrilled Isaiah recognized Preston. Preston talked to Isaiah a bit and presented him with a pile of notes of encouragement and prayers from the Furman University Fellowship of Christian Athletes. What a precious gift. I promised to read them to Isaiah later. Preston did his best to have a conversation with Isaiah even though it was mostly one-sided as Isaiah could not speak back to him. Isaiah nodded and smiled a lot.

Fifteen minutes or so into Preston's visit, I remembered that Abrianna had sent me a playlist she made Isaiah the day before. She sent it with specific instructions to play "Locked Away" by Maroon 5 for him. She told me it was his favorite song. I decided to go ahead and play it for him while Preston was there. Isaiah lit up and began mouthing the words to the song. He remembered! I played the song again, and he sang along. He sang with his voice. It was an incredible moment for me, Preston, Clarissa, and another nurse who was in the room. Before September 8, a moment like that would have meant little to me, but that day, I cherished every step back toward Isaiah's previous life.

I didn't understand, though, how he was able to sing but not speak. Clarissa informed me that the music part of the brain is different from the speaking part. It was at that moment I decided music would be a part of his healing.

I don't believe God wants any of us to struggle or suffer. That was never part of his original plan. God didn't do this to us, but I do know He was using it for His glory. Something I pulled from the box of peace God continued to hold for me was my view of what a tragedy truly is. In the past, I might have considered tragedy to be synonymous with loss. Yes, there had been loss, but right behind it came gifts we would never have expected amid such trials: peace in the midst of chaos, joy within sorrow, and even a path of light surrounded by darkness. For every bit of it, I am profoundly grateful.

Every day is a miracle. The next day, a Thursday, however, was extra special for me. I woke up from my nightly nap and sat up. I was watching Isaiah as he opened his eyes. The joy I continued to find in his movement would never get old. Then his mouth began moving, and he said, "Good morning." He actually said *good morning* with his voice! That might have been the best thing I heard all week. I felt the smile would jump off my face as I told him how great of a day it would be and how many wonderful things he was going to do. I told him he was strong and courageous and was not going to give up even when he was tired. I had a good feeling.

He went back to sleep until around eleven in the morning, when Laurie, the speech therapist, and Karla came into the room to work with him. Laurie asked Isaiah several questions to see if he could answer them and gave him some words and numbers he was to repeat. I felt chills all over. He answered almost every single one out loud. Laurie's eyes were wide and her smile broad. She giggled and laughed the whole time. She kept saying, "Pass." She was delighted to see him pass most of her tests and even surpass the level she expected him to. What a miracle!

Then Karla decided to take him on a field trip. She stood him up, strapped him into a wheelchair, and wheeled him to the other side of the pediatric floor to see the fish in the aquarium. It was the first time he had left the room since the previous Tuesday and the longest he had sat up. On our way down the hall, I played some music on my phone. He took the phone from my hand, then with his one functional hand, he refreshed it, swiped the screen to unlock it, and scrolled down the playlist to find the song he wanted to hear. He then chose the song, locked the screen, and handed it back to me.

What a miracle. I never thought a teenage technology addiction would make me so happy, but little things became monuments of joy.

Later, during dinner, my dad (his papa) tried to help him eat, but Isaiah wanted to do all of it by himself. Most impressive was watching Isaiah try to figure out how he could open a cup of pudding while holding a spoon with one hand. He was determined. After he figured out it was impossible, he let Papa hold the cup of pudding while he fed himself with a spoon for the first time with his left hand. What a miracle.

That night, because he was doing so well, they removed his heart monitor. I felt fear. For a moment, I worried about what might happen if something went wrong in the middle of the night. *What if I don't wake up? How will they know? What if he dies?* I had to check myself (before I wrecked myself) and remember I had trusted God ten days before as Isaiah lay on the operating table. I trusted God during those first crucial seventy-two hours. What was different about this day? Nothing. So I prayed God would help me trust Him again and allow me to sleep without worry. After praying, I knew I would sleep well with the knowledge that God loves Isaiah even more than I do, and He would keep watch while I closed my eyes to rest.

The words of this song from Lamentations 3:22–24 (ESV) came to mind: "The steadfast love of the Lord never ceases; his mercies never come to an end; they are new every morning; great is your faithfulness. 'The Lord is my portion,' says my soul, 'therefore I will hope in him.'"

CHAPTER 6

THE BLANKET TENT

Sometimes you just have to cover your head and make a tent out of your blanket.

The next morning, Isaiah woke up not feeling well. He was touching his head while his face showed he was in extreme pain, and he kept asking to go home. When someone has had a brain bleed and experiences intense head pain, the medical staff wastes no time. They decided to do a CT scan.

That fear came sneaking back. *Breathe, Christina. You can trust God.* Even though I kept reminding myself I could trust God, I trembled. The staff allowed me to go down with Isaiah as he seemed nervous. I felt the same. He kept calling out to me, making sure I was with him. That only increased my anxiety. My mother's intuition alarm was wailing, and my stomach felt as if it were turning inside out.

The test didn't take long, and we received the results quickly. The scan came back clear. I could breathe normally again. After a process of elimination, the doctor on call figured out that Isaiah's pain was the direct result of not moving his bowels in over a week.

My mind went from the depth of bowel matters to matters of the spirit. It was like God smacked me with a lesson. Our bowels are like the issues in our lives. We hold on to so much pain. We cling to anger, frustration, unforgiveness, jealousy, and so on. All that waste. All that junk causing us so much pain, loss of sleep, and sometimes health problems. If we would only "dump" those things and give them over to God, the pain would end. We would find relief. Sometimes it's a matter of finally telling someone we are in pain, then asking for help.

Yes. Yes, I did find spiritual application from my baby's bowels. Isaiah was eventually able to handle his business and find rest. God shows up to teach me in every kind of situation—even in the bathroom.

That night I looked forward to laying my head on a pillow and drifting off to sleep as I contemplated the mysteries of God. Isaiah had different plans. He put them into action in the wee hours of Saturday morning. He was determined to get out of bed. I stepped in front of the bed, blocking his way. He'd tried to get up before, but this time he was going to push me out of the way to get there. He looked at me. His jaw was set, and his eyes narrowed. He had formulated a plan, and no one was going to stop him. I had to get stern.

I felt the frustration one experiences with a newborn when you've just gone into a deep sleep and they wake you up with a piercing scream—and it continued for hours. I don't know what came over him. He wouldn't sleep. It was as if some kind of spirit came over him and hijacked his need for sleep.

I thought back to Isaiah as a baby. There were several times I would get him into his car seat, and he refused to stay. He would bow his body, making it impossible to strap him in. He would squirm, scream, and kick, fighting me with everything he had in him. After a few times of that happening, I decided it would take a much higher power to resolve the situation. I put my palm on his little forehead and shouted, "In the name of Jesus, spirit, come out of Isaiah." I kid you not—his body immediately relaxed, and he settled into his car seat. To be honest, it's not what I expected, and I was half kidding, but wow! Okay, I was a little freaked out.

Now, in the hospital, it crossed my mind again to call out that same spirit. But Isaiah was bigger this time, and I imagined the spirit was too. So I left it alone.

We finally made it to the reasonable hours of that Saturday morning, but Isaiah was still agitated and wanted to get out of bed. He kept asking, "Why?" Neither the medical staff nor I was sure if that's what he meant to say or if he were trying to communicate something else. Whatever it was, it broke our hearts. We weren't getting it.

I asked the nurse to please bring a wheelchair and help me get him out of bed. Isaiah groaned in frustration and cried without tears. He physically agreed to go but then changed his mind and wanted to get back in bed and stay there. I made him sit in the chair and take that ride. He tried to push me out of the way because I was in his face. I refused to take it personally. I told him to stop pushing me, then moved even closer to his face and sternly told him he was going to do this. I let him know I was sorry he was upset and frustrated and that it was okay to cry. I would cry too. But it was time to sit up, be strong, and push through it.

I asked him who was inside him, and he said, "Me." I told him he was there but so was Jesus, and he could do all things through Christ who strengthens him, so he could do this.

Then I cried a little.

We strapped him to the wheelchair, and with one hand, he grabbed the Ohio State blanket my brother Jonathan had given him and put it over his head. He left that blanket on his head the whole way down the hall, and there it stayed as we sat in front of the giant aquarium. He cared nothing about the creepy fish staring at him or the nurses wondering why he was hiding. I took a couple of minutes to enjoy the creatures in the water myself. After a few minutes, we took him back to the room and still made him sit in the chair. I told him he was going to sit there a little longer because I wasn't going to let him give up and lie in bed all day! I wanted to add, "'Cuz I'm straight outta Compton!" But I'm not, so that would have been ridiculous.

I finally let him get back in bed, and he went right to sleep. We had exhausted him. Some of the tension that had been building up inside of me subsided. He was finally still, and he napped for a long time. I remembered that when your baby sleeps is when you should sleep. I couldn't sleep. I was still on watch.

Around the time he started to wake up, his nurse came and told us it was time for him to move to a regular room. Insurance required him to stay in a standard room for at least two days before moving to rehab. Rehab! He was doing so well, and the medical staff thought he was ready. I had mixed feelings about that because the staff in the PICU absolutely spoils their patients. Each nurse cares for only one or two patients, so they are almost always available. We had been there for twelve days, and it felt comfortable and safe. I had no idea what it would be like in the "real world" of a standard room. Would the nurses be as attentive? Would they care about Isaiah as much as the PICU nurses did? I had to pray my fear away. I still worried he could die if no one monitored him closely.

I called Ozzy to let him know what was happening, and he left work to help us with the transition. That afternoon we packed up all Isaiah's cards, balloons, flowers, blankets, and items proving he was loved and headed to another part of the hospital. When we arrived at his regular room, my now-wide eyes scanned our new space. *Seriously, God? More blessings?* I know it's silly, but I felt as though we had cashed in our reward points and received an upgrade. We were in a corner room with a wall of windows and a ton more room. I guess we could handle it for a couple of days. Two days would give us—well, me—time to mentally prepare for the rehabilitation facility where things would get serious (as if twelve days in the PICU weren't serious already).

Once we settled into our new room, Isaiah was in good spirits and accepted a few visitors. His smiles and hugs were readily available, and he even threw out an "I love you" to our friends Angie and Adrianna. At least Ozzy and I think that's what he said.

It had been a long day. That night, through hand motions, Isaiah let us know he had to go to the bathroom, and he went! His colon was flowing. Because of that small victory, Isaiah's doctor decided he would not have to do a procedure to drain his brain of extra blood and fluids. The morning's struggle and tears were wiped away by the blessing of calm in the evening. Although the times of day are different, this verse came to mind: "Weeping may endure for a night, but joy cometh in the morning" (Psalm 30:5 KJV).

The next day was Sunday and the thirteenth day of our stay. We had a relatively quiet morning, and friends came to visit. It was terrific to see Isaiah's personality come out when he "talked" with his friends. He even joked around some and smiled a lot. He would point and laugh and shake his head as he used his facial expressions to poke fun.

He didn't get to rest before his PT session, but he did so well. He proved he was ready for real rehab. As he was finishing his session, Ozzy came to the hospital with the girls. They had been to church together, which was nice because the girls hadn't had much time with their dad. If he wasn't at work, he was at the hospital with Isaiah and me.

After PT, we had Isaiah sit up in a wheelchair. Then Ozzy, Olivia, and I wheeled him around. He visited his nurse friends in the PICU, and then we went down to the healing garden, where they were having a carnival for the kids in the hospital. It took every ounce of strength and cheering from Ozzy and me to get Isaiah to throw a ball at the dunk tank. He was still weak and struggled to reach the target as he would have before. The frustration was apparent by the way he was twisting up his face, but we encouraged him to keep trying. Finally, with great effort, he landed the ball on the target, and the man inside went down. The working side of his face lit up, and Isaiah gave a crooked smile. He enjoyed listening to a band for a few minutes but tired very quickly, so we left and returned to his room.

Soon after getting back in bed, some familiar figures appeared at the door. I looked up and smiled. Then I worried that Isaiah wouldn't know who they were. My fears were quickly put to rest when Isaiah's eyes found the door and his face lit up. It was his football coaches, whom he loved and respected so much.

A twinge of sadness pricked me as I flashed forward to a future I believed was taken from him. We never had a chance to go to that first game where he would have played with a team that wasn't just recreational ball but the beginning of his high school football career. In that moment, I pictured him bent over with his hand on a football, surrounded by an army of orange jerseys. I heard someone behind him yelling whatever those words are the guy behind the guy holding the ball yells. I imagined him snapping the ball, then running toward another big kid with great intention, wrapping his arms around him, and taking him down hard.

When Isaiah was little, I never wanted him to play football. I feared watching him get hurt on the field. It was what most mothers fear, but I had finally embraced it when I could see how much he loved it and how good he was at it. I trusted God to take care of him. Besides, he was bigger than most of those kids. I wasn't the mother who needed to be afraid. But now, who knew what his new future would be?

I didn't, but God sure did.

The presence of these men who had begun to shape Isaiah into a different kind of young man—an athlete—made Isaiah feel like part of the team again. He felt normal. Then they left, and reality came crashing down again. Their arrival, then departure reminded us of a new normal. We didn't want it. We were afraid of it. It was in front of us, nevertheless. Maybe if I put a blanket over my head, it would go away.

CHAPTER 7

HANGING ON THE EDGE

No good day goes unpunished. Sunday night was the worst ever. Isaiah was agitated by everything: light, dark, covers, no covers, pillow, Mom, no Mom, people talking—everything!

It was Monday, and everything was *not* awesome. I hit the wall of exhaustion, and if you wanted to buy tickets to see me cry, you could have gotten a good show. On a positive note, all of Isaiah's aggravation was more than likely a sign he was becoming more aware and healing. I heard him say things that fit a particular situation. "When will stop?" "Where is it?" "Why?" Those questions made me so sad, but I reminded my heart that they showed his brain was engaging with his situation. As I cried, I held on to this Scripture passage:

> Come to me, all you who are weary and burdened, and I will give you rest. Take my yoke upon you and learn from me, for I am gentle and humble in heart, and you will find rest for your souls. For my yoke is easy and my burden is light. (Matthew 11:28–30)

That Monday morning, Isaiah and I were enjoying breakfast together when Ozzy showed up at the door. He often came by the hospital before going to work to check in and give us some love.

Not too long after he arrived, a nurse walked in with a big smile. "I'm here to take out your staples."

My heart pounded. *What? Just like that? We don't even have time to prepare.* I asked her if she would give him lidocaine to numb the part of his head where the staples were. I was concerned about the level of pain he was about to endure. She smiled again. "This shouldn't hurt at all." She then launched right into the staple removal with her tool of torment and pulled out the first one.

Isaiah gasped and let out a blood-curdling scream. "No-o-o!"

The nurse continued to yank each staple out one by one as Isaiah screamed. She looked perplexed. "It shouldn't hurt."

My eyes narrowed as Isaiah sobbed. *Clearly, it does, and if you don't hurry up, you might catch a throat punch.*

She finally pulled out the last staple, gathered her torture device, and cleared away the pile of bloody staples. I let her leave in silence, also silently wishing I could extend my foot and trip her on her way out the door. *Forgive me, Lord.*

It was finished. I crawled into Isaiah's bed and wrapped my arms around him as he cried himself to sleep. On the plus side, the staples were out, and he could finally get a good haircut. I was over the post-brain-surgery look. Ozzy stayed a little longer and helped Isaiah get a real shower. I was grateful for his support.

Later that afternoon, I packed up our things and put Isaiah in a wheelchair, then together we waited for hospital transport to take us to another part of the hospital called Roger C. Peace Rehabilitation Hospital (RCP). I was excited but nervous for Isaiah. From what I had heard, rehab would be one of the most challenging and physically painful parts of his journey. His nurse Jessica told us we could expect to be there around three weeks, so I mentally prepared for our three-week pilgrimage.

Transport came and took us to our new room. It wasn't as spacious as where we had been for two days, but it would be fine. I began decorating right away. Encouraging posters went up on the wall. I taped every card Isaiah had received all over the room. I set various gifts friends gave him on a little dresser-type area. I even set up my little chair-bed area to look like a regular bed covered with the precious green blanket embroidered with a *W* from my friend Arlyn that had become a cloak of comfort during a difficult night. That room would be our home for almost a month. I needed it to feel like one.

Tuesday morning had me searching for a reset button. We were in our new room and adjusting to the new atmosphere. Nurses wouldn't be coming to check on him so often, and I had rules to learn about my role in this new place. They told me I had to call for help anytime Isaiah needed to go to the bathroom or needed anything. He was still wearing adult diapers, but we were teaching him to use an actual toilet again.

Later that morning was one of those times. He had successfully used the portable commode next to his bed. He finished, and I called for a nurse assistant to help him back to bed. It took a while, but she finally came. She turned around while she was adjusting and preparing the bed for Isaiah to get back in. Isaiah decided it was time to get off the commode and that the nurse assistant wasn't moving fast enough. Before either of us noticed the wheels turning in his head, he fixed his eyes and leaped toward the bed.

He didn't make it. It was a scene similar to the beginning of the movie *Mission: Impossible II*, where Tom Cruise intentionally and elegantly hangs from the edge of a cliff, except without the intentionality and elegance. Also, visualize replacing Tom Cruise with a frog of some sort, straining to pull himself up with one arm. I hurried to grab Isaiah to make sure he didn't fall to the floor. I couldn't get him up. One hundred and eighty pounds of dead weight was too much for me. I did, however, manage to get in his face to tell him to remember how he felt at that moment and next time wait for help.

Then I told him he was grounded.

It was the first day of occupational therapy (OT), PT, speech therapy, and a meeting with the neuropsychologist. The rehab hospital required me to be there for it all. Regardless of the requirement, I wouldn't have missed a moment. That place and my kid were my primary focus.

I mentioned to Shawn, the physical therapist, that I anticipated Isaiah would walk out of the hospital. Isaiah was determined and pushed himself hard. I even caught him smiling when his right leg moved a little during PT. It was awesome. I told him that he and

I would work hard together and that I was so thankful I could do all of it with him.

He gave me a blank look. "Party."

Then later—heartbreak. Soon after we made it back to our room, the nurse told me that the psychologist wanted to talk to me privately. I told Isaiah to take a nap, and I would be back shortly. I headed down the hall, feeling optimistic, looking forward to learning some things about Isaiah's situation and hopefully finding encouragement concerning his future.

The meeting was okay. The neuropsychologist, Dr. Cozbi, seemed very sure of the information she was giving me even though she didn't typically deal with children. Like other doctors we had talked to, she agreed that his recovery would take six to twelve months and that change after that time was unlikely.

I looked around her office and spotted her medical degree. I didn't see the "Lord God Almighty" signature anywhere on that framed piece of paper, so I took what she said with a grain of salt. I told her what a great kid Isaiah was and that I believed God would do amazing things with and for him. He would be doing more than the medical staff ever expected in a short period of time.

She smiled and told me it was nice that I had faith. I sensed condescension.

I tensed up and decided to moderate my thoughts and words and simply say thank you, then get back to my boy. I stood up. I was done with her. I hadn't received much encouragement, but it didn't matter. I trusted a God who always provided what I needed.

I decided at that moment, I would wholeheartedly trust what God was telling me. The medical staff kept telling me I should expect his recovery to take six months to a year. I had such a difficult time accepting that time frame because my God is bigger than any medical diagnosis or prognosis. I would consider what the doctors told me, but I knew God had given me an extra sense of what I needed to do for my son. From the beginning of his life, I had known that I needed to be on special alert, and nothing had changed.

By the time I came back fifteen minutes later, Isaiah was sitting straight up in the bed, crying his eyes out. I didn't know how long he had been like that, but I put my arms around him, and he wrapped his around me, then cried and cried. He had needed to go to the bathroom, and I wasn't there for him.

His new rehab doctor, Dr. Soberon, had classified his room as "low stimulation." That meant only two visitors at a time and little noise. They also said that the number of visitors he should have in a day should be limited. That is typical for a patient with a brain injury. *Is the crying thing typical too? How long will we be dealing with this?* Then I remembered my trust commitment—my God is bigger.

Various nurses and therapists told us we needed to adjust things in our house so that Isaiah could get around—things like adding handrails, converting the dining room to a bedroom, putting a shower in the garage. They didn't expect him to be able to go up and down stairs, even after he left the hospital. That's a lot of adjusting. So much, in fact, that it made me consider moving to a more suitable home. Their lack of faith in what Isaiah would be able to do gave me moments of discouragement, but I knew something they didn't—my God is bigger.

Wednesday morning, therapies went well, and Isaiah was in a reasonably good mood. He had been up several times the night before but only to go to the bathroom. He went right back to sleep each time. That was an improvement. Best of all, my brother, Anthony, came from Ohio. Isaiah was glad to see him and agreed to let him cut his hair the next day. The I-just-had-brain-surgery look was not working for him.

That day Isaiah's new speech therapist, Carey, fell in love with him. He had played her some of his favorite songs from a Spotify playlist, and he sang along. She let him know she was too old for him but that she loved him. I figured that would happen. He has that effect on women.

His PT session took place in our room, and since Shawn was there, I felt comfortable leaving Isaiah under his care. Margie, the recreational therapist, wanted to talk to me in her office to learn more about Isaiah. I loved her! She was sweet and enthusiastic. I could have talked and planned with her all day. About twenty minutes into our conversation, Shawn came in to tell me Isaiah was upset and that I needed to come back. It had happened again. I found him sobbing and needing some serious mom comfort. The situation exacerbated my feeling that I could never leave him. But I had to.

It seemed that, even when he was distressed, he was okay as long as I was there in front of him, telling him he could do it and to be strong. A couple of older and wiser nurses explained how he could end up with an unhealthy dependency on me, so I knew we would have to go through a weaning process. That wasn't easy. He was thirteen years old but still my baby boy.

As I held him in my arms, I explained to him, "Isaiah, I know it feels scary when I am away, but sometimes I'm going to have to leave, and I need you to be okay. You are strong, and you can do this."

He cried and said, "No."

I felt something inside me break, but I sat up and shifted so he could look directly into my eyes.

"Isaiah, it won't be today, but one day I'm going to have to go somewhere without you, and you are going to be just fine."

He looked at me with a blank stare and tears streaming down his face. I don't think he was convinced. That's okay. Neither was I.

I think both of us felt we were standing on the edge of a cliff.

PART 2

GOD AT WORK WITHIN US

CHAPTER 8

SUSTENANCE

Every day Isaiah showed improvement, and every day my faith increased. Many of the medical professionals we dealt with told us initially it could be days between seeing any changes, but they didn't take into account who our God is. His healing was coming fast and furious. I had finally reached a point where I believed with my whole heart that God would let us keep Isaiah. I was finally sleeping at night. Why did it take me so long? I finally remembered God's Word:

> You are the God who performs miracles; you display your power among the peoples. (Psalm 77:14)

> I am the Lord, the God of all mankind. Is anything too hard for me? (Jeremiah 32:27)

> For I am the Lord, who heals you. (Exodus 15:26)

Thursday started with nothing less than a small miracle. Isaiah's speech had primarily consisted of the words *yeah, no,* and *when.* Remember the movie *Guardians of the Galaxy* where Groot's character could only say, "I am Groot"? Well, Isaiah was our Groot. He especially fixated on the word *when.* He constructed whole sentences out of that one word. So we had to try and translate that word into whatever he wanted to tell us. It was highly frustrating for all of us. Even if you asked him his name, he would say, "When." This morning, however, he woke up before dawn, looked at me, and said, "Hungry."

Hungry!

Unfortunately, breakfast wouldn't come for at least an hour and a half. That meant I was sentenced to be up in that five o'clock hour right along with Isaiah. He was wide awake and wanted to watch TV. So that's what we did until right before breakfast when he said, "Turn it off," then fell asleep.

Groot can speak!

Isaiah's first therapy of the day was OT. His therapist, Reagan, used a vibrating wand to "wake up" his muscles, and he was able to lift his right arm all the way up. He couldn't do that the day before.

Later, while he was with Carey, he identified all kinds of words by reading them aloud. She was amazed. My baby could read. He could also say his name when asked. He couldn't do that the day before.

Later, he met with Shawn, where he lifted and moved his right leg three different ways. I was thrilled. My happy heart did all kinds of somersaults. I was expecting PT to be the worst, most grueling, most heartbreaking thing about being there. I expected weeping and gnashing of teeth, but Isaiah smiled almost the whole time. He was moving his leg and didn't care how much it hurt. He was moving his leg! He couldn't do that the day before.

Shawn was thrilled, and he and I both couldn't help but smile at Isaiah's joy. I told Isaiah that a few hundred more people must have joined us in prayer because he'd had a miraculous day.

That afternoon I thought about how Isaiah had exhibited such patience and determination through our whole journey. I never saw him get angry that he couldn't move his right side. He simply took his left hand and lifted his right with it. He did the same with his legs. He also hooked his left foot under his right foot to move it. Shawn said Isaiah's was not a typical reaction to the loss of movement. Most people either give up or try to fling their arms or legs around to get them to do what they want.

Don't you wish we could be the same way with each other? I often get so impatient with those who seem weak-minded or so damaged that they can't seem to do anything right for their lives. I know how hard it can be when we get so caught up in our own stuff that we don't have the time or patience to help someone unable to help themselves. Well, Paul said in Romans 15:1, "We who are strong ought to bear with the failings of the weak and not to please ourselves."

Through his weakness, Isaiah was teaching me. He was helping me find joy in activities I took for granted before. He was teaching me patience (although I still had to work on being patient with the nurses' response time). I am so grateful God chose me to be his mom. What an awesome responsibility. What an awesome God, who sustains us.

"Breakfast." That was Isaiah's first word Friday morning. He woke up early again and wanted to be fed. The appetite that kid had was incredible. The next thing he said was, "When?"

When?

"Ask her when."

Since I knew he was hungry, I deduced that he wanted me to ask the nurse when breakfast was coming. I tried not to freak out and scream or jump up and down when he said things like that (I needed to stay #coollikeisaiah, as his social media followers would say), but I was jumping up and down inside. Every day he said more and more. His progress was unbelievable.

But then there was the issue of dependence.

Many people gave me advice about whether or not I should wean Isaiah from my constant presence. Most felt I shouldn't worry about it and let him continue to depend on me. In my spirit, however, I truly felt his dependency was not a good thing. It wasn't healthy for either of us for me to be with him every second of the day. He couldn't seem to cope with any challenging situation without me being there. It wasn't good for him. His success did not depend on my presence, and he needed to know he had it within him to accomplish anything. He needed to remember that he always had Jesus.

It was September 25, and I had only seen the light of day twice since September 8, and I had started to get a twitch. I'm not kidding. So I left that morning—for three whole hours.

I did not leave Isaiah alone. I left him with the next best thing: my mother. He became teary-eyed a whole hour before I left, but I assured him I would be back and reminded him I wasn't leaving him alone. I told him he was strong and courageous, and he could do anything without me for a little while. I kissed him goodbye, then went and spent much-needed girl time with some friends.

I was proud of me.

When I returned from my outing, Isaiah was taking a nap. My mom reported that he did great in his therapy sessions. He especially rocked PT. He stood on both legs for about a minute a few times, then did a partial squat. Seriously, I can barely do one squat with two functioning legs. Also, during speech therapy, he wrote his name. He is right-handed, so I was impressed he was able to do that with his left hand. This time, my heart did a cartwheel, finishing off the celebration with a backflip roundhouse.

When he woke up, I asked him how his morning had been, and he said, "Good." He agreed he could stay in the hospital without me sometimes and understood that I would always return. He also expressed that being without me for a little while wasn't as bad as he thought it would be.

When I was there for his second PT session, Shawn told me that Isaiah had done three different therapies in one session. I think he had stepped up the game for Isaiah. I reminded him that Ozzy and my goal for Isaiah was not only to walk out of RCP but to be able to ascend and descend stairs. The first day of therapy, only three days before, he had seemed hesitant to say he could get Isaiah there, but that day it seemed as if he had a change of heart. He appeared extraordinarily excited about Isaiah's progress and pushed him hard.

Friday was Anthony's last day in town with us. What a blessing he had been. He had showed up and jumped right into the craziness of our lives and could even keep up. He assisted my mom in the surrogate motherhood of Abrianna and Olivia. He picked up, dropped off, sat and watched, ran around, and at the end of it all, continued to ask, "How can I help?" (Yes, ladies, he is single.) Anthony's presence meant a great deal to Isaiah, whose eyes lit up when he saw him and dimmed when he left that night.

As I wound down that night and reflected on the day, I thought about my visit with friends that morning. My friend Chris said I seemed good and refreshed, and I must have been getting more sleep. I told her I hadn't had much more sleep, but I was taking a good supplement, along with being revived and refreshed through the power of prayer.

Though I felt okay, there was still a weariness inside of me. I wondered how long the hospital would be my home. I was faithful but still uncertain God would restore Isaiah to what he was before that life-changing September night. I learned that the saying "God doesn't give you anything you can't handle" is not true and is not found in the Bible. We can't handle everything. We just can't. That's precisely what Philippians 4:13 (NLT) means when it says, "For I can do everything through Christ, who gives me strength." That is the truth to hold on to, especially in situations like ours.

What we were going through had Jesus all over it. God blessed me with such peace and rest in Him. That's the only explanation for how I could function and even speak in complete sentences during that time. One of my favorite Scriptures explains God's providence perfectly. It also explains Isaiah's journey of recovery:

> Do you not know?
> Have you not heard?
> The Lord is the everlasting God,
> the Creator of the ends of the earth.
> He will not grow tired or weary,
> and his understanding no one can fathom.
> He gives strength to the weary
> and increases the power of the weak.
> Even youths grow tired and weary,
> and young men stumble and fall;
> but those who hope in the Lord
> will renew their strength.
> They will soar on wings like eagles;
> they will run and not grow weary,
> they will walk and not be faint. (Isaiah 40:28–31)

I was counting on God to get me to the next chapter of our lives. I depended on Him to continue to carry me when I felt I couldn't stand. Through my gratitude, I cried and feared the next day could bring disappointment.

CHAPTER 9

CHRISTLIKE FRAGRANCE

I woke up Saturday morning with an increase in energy. Isaiah had only been up only one time to go to the bathroom, so we had actually slept. This morning, however, he was super grumpy and hangry. Dr. Soberon came into our room bright and early and woke him up. He looked at her through squinted eyes and said, "No-o! Go away. Go away!"

I understood how he felt, but also told him it was not okay to be rude. His not-so-sunny disposition continued through OT, then during speech therapy. He constantly looked at the clock and kept rushing Carey through her questions, and in the middle of their session, he said, "Bathroom." I told him I would take him to the bathroom, but he would have to come back to finish. I asked him if he still wanted to go.

He looked annoyed. "No." He sighed, then turned back to do his work. Smart kid.

PT was a struggle as well. He hung his head and looked sad. Shawn and I questioned him about what was wrong, asking if he was just tired, but it seemed more like sadness to me. He pointed to his head, so we asked if he had a headache.

He nodded yes.

I looked at him skeptically. "Tell the truth."

He looked back with guilty eyes. "No."

He was trying to get out of therapy. Smart kid.

He made it through PT okay but lay down for a nap when we returned to our room. He woke up a little while later when he heard the voices of visitors. My dad had come and brought Abrianna. Isaiah's mood changed and he became smiley. I didn't know what his earlier problem was, but I was thankful he had found his way back to his normal self.

After thirty minutes of hanging out, I pulled out a new pack of UNO cards, shuffled them, then set them down on Isaiah's lap while I turned to do something. When I turned back around, Isaiah had the cards in one hand and dealt seven cards to each of us. He couldn't say seven, but he could count to it. He set the whole game up by himself. I was elated. I played the first two games with them, then took a nap in the bed next to his. Isaiah, Abrianna, and my dad played for at least another hour. *It's funny how the tiniest things are now so monumental.*

A feeling struck me around nine o'clock that night to find a couple somewhere down the hall whom my friend Sarah had told me about. Brent and Linda were friends of her family. Linda was at RCP because she had suffered a stroke and was also fighting cancer. I had met Brent briefly when Sarah's husband Geoff was visiting and saw them in the hall, but we didn't have a whole conversation.

I generally have a tough time putting myself out there to meet people, but I felt so drawn to these strangers for some reason. I found the room they were in and stood in front of the door. Brent looked up and saw me, then invited me in. Long story short, I was there for over an hour, getting to know them and their story and sharing mine and Isaiah's with them.

They were strong believers, and as they shared their lives with me, I felt chills all over. I knew we ended up a few rooms apart for a reason. It was not a coincidence. Isaiah and I had something to learn from their journey—and they from ours.

So many blessings wait around the corner if we will only take a chance to go there. God speaks to us every day—even those who claim to have no relationship with God—but so many times we don't listen. He wants a relationship with all of us, so I know He speaks to and even through every single one of us. I decided I would continue doing my best to hear what God was trying to tell me each day.

—⁓—

"Hungry, hungry, hungryyyy!"

Those are the sounds I woke up to at 3:48 a.m. Sunday, and I was not happy. Although I was thankful Isaiah was alive and able to speak that word, I was also highly irritated with his presentation and the time he chose to present. I grudgingly removed myself from the bed, grabbed not one but two bananas, peeled them, and handed them to him. He practically inhaled them. I lay down and went back to sleep until 3:57 a.m.

"Hungryy . . . hungryy . . . huungryy . . ."

Oh my gosh. "How in the world can you be hungry?" I begged him to go back to sleep, but he refused. I almost expected him to say, "Feed me, Seymour!" Around four o'clock, his nurse Jarvis entered the room.

I looked at the nurse with desperation. "He's hungry. I already gave him two bananas. I don't know what to do."

Jarvis said he'd be right back. *All hail nurse Jarvis!* He returned with a large ham sandwich, a cup of yogurt, and some graham crackers with peanut butter. I almost cried tears of joy, and I thanked him profusely. Isaiah downed that sandwich, yogurt, and two of the graham crackers. Then he finally went back to sleep. It took me a while to get back to sleep because I lay there in disbelief, thinking about my caveman of a son. I prayed it was just a growth spurt. Because if the appetite part of his brain had been affected, we were going to have serious issues.

He later woke up at a normal time for waking up and asked for breakfast. Thank goodness it had just arrived.

After breakfast, he was very antsy and wanted to go out. I asked him if he knew it was Sunday, and he said, "Yes."

"We need to talk to God before we start our day." I prayed first, then asked him if he wanted to pray. He told me no. I instinctively understood why. I assured him it would be okay and that God would understand what he was saying.

He started with "God, thank you." He was about to say more but quickly became frustrated because he couldn't get the words out. I told him to continue because God knew what he was saying. The only thing I could understand was thank you. He said it all through the prayer, along with other things I didn't understand, but it may have been one of the most precious prayers I've ever heard.

Sunday was the only day of the week he had no therapy, so we had lots of time to do what we wanted. I packed him up in his wheelchair, and we went outside to the healing garden. Immediately, a beautiful look of peace came across his face, and he smiled.

"Does it feel good out here, Isaiah?"

He took a deep breath. "Yes."

It was drizzling and a bit chilly, so we didn't stay out long. But it was nice to be out of the rehabilitation wing of the hospital. We walked through the main hospital and then again felt drawn back outside to the healing garden. It was quiet and beautiful there. Isaiah and I both agreed we could sense God. A little while later, we met my parents and went to the Starbucks inside the hospital. My mom, Isaiah, and I chatted while my dad fell asleep in a chair.

Some things never change.

When I saw Isaiah getting tired, I took him back up to our room. He slept a little while, then later woke up to visit with some family members who had come. It was Ozzy's brother and his family. My sister-in-law, Sandee, had a surprise. She had dyed her hair blue in honor of Isaiah. My brother-in-law Eddie didn't show up empty-handed. He brought *arroz con leche* (rice pudding). That made Isaiah's day and put a big smile on his face. It was his favorite. Later, he was delighted to visit with two of his loyal friends and teammates, Dominic and Bryson. That day, I almost forgot why we were there. Almost.

Monday started like the four previous days—with my caveman waking up hungry. Although it was closer to a normal time at six o'clock, it was still an hour and a half before breakfast would come. So I reluctantly rose from the bed, handed him a banana, and gave him the rest of the *arroz con leche*. Unfortunately, that wasn't enough.

But never fear—*dun-dun-dun-duuun*! Jarvis is here! Jarvis was ready this time. He had two sandwiches prepared and was waiting for Isaiah to wake up. Seriously. That guy is my hero.

After Isaiah ate his "snack," we went back to sleep. Apparently, we slept too late because Isaiah's "favorite" doctor, Dr. Soberon, came in and semi-reprimanded us about how late it was. So we roused ourselves and started our day.

Isaiah had a hard time getting himself together that morning for therapy. I think he had hit a point where he was so tired of being there that all he could think about was going home. I had to explain that the only way we would get out of there was if he worked super hard and walked out. He did well in PT but became fatigued and dizzy at times. Shawn had him standing up on both feet, then supporting his weight with his right leg and moving his left leg back. That was a significant accomplishment.

OT also went very well. The best moment was when I had Isaiah choose some music that would motivate him. He chose "Watch Me," then proceeded to whip and nae nae in his wheelchair. He sang and danced hard during the whole song. Reagan and I and everyone else around stopped what we were doing and cracked up laughing as we watched. He was so happy. He danced like no one was watching.

Next was speech therapy. We had to wait because Carey wasn't in her office. While we were sitting there waiting, Isaiah said, "I don't think she's coming." Wow! That was a big sentence for him! She eventually came, and Isaiah continued to impress her with the quality of his speech. What did not impress her was at the end of his second session when he decided to lift up in his chair and pollute the air with the stench of his last digested meal. I was embarrassed. Carey was shocked. She couldn't believe the sweet, precious boy she had fallen in love with the previous week could do such a thing. He apologized, followed by deep laughter. My Isaiah was back.

Our friend Don from church blessed us with his musical talents that night. Isaiah was all smiles and sang along. I considered it a therapy session. Later, we enjoyed the company of Mauldin's booster club president and his wife, who presented Isaiah with a football game jersey. Before they left, they asked if there was anything we needed or anything they or the community could do. Isaiah said yes. Then he did his best to share his thoughts. He did so well with the words, along with his hand motions, that I finally understood what he wanted to tell them. He was thankful for all they had done for him (the pictures, the messages, the visits, etc.) and wanted them to know he was fighting to get better and was thankful for all the prayers. I think we may have seen a small preview of his first speaking engagement.

The night concluded with lots of laughter as Ozzy, Abrianna, Olivia, Isaiah, and I were all together. It was nice to have all five of us together in the same room. Isaiah kept things light with his sense of humor—and stinky as he answered "the call of the wild burrito" as I like to call it. He couldn't seem to get his gas under control.

The funny thing is that my son still managed to help me see God, even in all his stinky glory. Isaiah was so pleased with himself and his back-end blowout. He didn't care what it smelled like to the rest of us. It made me think of 2 Corinthians 2:15 (NLT): "Our lives are a Christ-like fragrance rising up to God. But this fragrance is perceived differently by those who are being saved and by those who are perishing." Isaiah's "manly" fragrance was certainly not one I would offer up to the Lord, but I do pray that Isaiah continues to live his life in a way that his Christlike fragrance rises and pleases the Lord.

I want the same for the rest of our family and myself. There have been times when I can't say my life represented Christ at all. One of the things I have prayed the most for us is that our lives honor God. We must first take time to step back and examine our lives and ask if anyone can see Christ in us. If not, then it's time to make a change.

On the night Isaiah almost died, we promised that if God allowed Isaiah to live, we would use his life to honor and glorify Him. The next few days would bring trials, but we remembered our vow and were doing our best.

CHAPTER 10

REJOICING IN TRIALS

Hallelujah! Isaiah slept until half-past seven Tuesday morning. I had to give props to Monday night's nurse, Karen. She was ready with a sandwich and snacks in case he woke up hangry.

I had a doctor's appointment that morning, so my mom came to hang with her grandson while I went. Afterward, Mom told me that Isaiah had been tired and didn't want to do therapy, but he did it anyway. Speech therapy was okay, but he wasn't into it. Carey did mention to my mom that she had needed to spray some air freshener after Isaiah left the room the previous day. So embarrassing.

When I came back from my appointment, Isaiah was asleep. I watched him for a while, the way I used to when he was a baby. When he woke up, I said hi and bent down to hug him. He put his arm around me and wouldn't let go for a while. I asked him if he was really tired or was just sad I hadn't been there. He said he was sad. Break my heart.

I told him it was important to have a good attitude and work hard even if I wasn't there. He said, "Okay." But he said okay to almost everything I told him, then would do what he wanted anyway. He was impulsive. Dr. Soberon said this effect was from a part of his brain that hadn't healed, not solely because he was thirteen. I wondered how long that impulsivity would last.

In OT, Reagan and I decided to make dancing part of his therapy. Once again, he entertained the room with his whip and nae nae skills. He's got a fantastic stanky legg.

Music is such a gift. After his last therapy session of the day, he asked to "Go."

"Where do you want to go, Isaiah?"

"Anywhere."

I knew his youth minister, Charlie, was coming later, but we went outside for a bit. We had been outside only a short while when Charlie called my cell phone to let me know he was there at the hospital. We met him at the hospital Starbucks, where Isaiah seemed even more like his old self as he joked and laughed with Charlie. We went back to our room, where Isaiah settled in, then visited with some friends.

From that time on, he became gastronomically expressive, and it only worsened after Ozzy brought him a burrito from Moe's. Have you ever had a feeling your husband and son were plotting against you? Ozzy had answered the call of the wild burrito.

Later in the day, Isaiah's caseworker, Christine, came in to tell me that our insurance company had approved RCP to keep Isaiah for another week beyond what they initially planned. She said it wasn't because he wasn't progressing, but the facility does that so they have more preapproved time if they need it. They want to keep him as long as possible so he gets all the time and attention he needs to recover.

Truthfully, that news was hard for me to take. I mean, I had it set in my mind that we would be there for three weeks. We had one down already and two to go. I now was looking at three more weeks. *Three more weeks.* It was getting old. I could stay optimistic about Isaiah's recovery and all that God was doing with his story, but the scenery was starting to get to me. Every day Isaiah would ask when we could leave, and every day I told him that if he worked hard, we'd be able to leave sooner. This time I told him that we had to be there for three more weeks.

He scrunched up his face. "Three weeks? *Ugh!*"

I felt his pain.

But when I looked back at the first days, I was reminded of how far he had come in exactly three weeks. It was at almost that time three weeks before when a sweet nurse called me from Isaiah's operating room to give me an update on his surgery. I remembered how she prayed with me over the phone. Wow. Only in the weeks after we made it through Isaiah's most critical moments was I able to absorb the complete miracle. We had come so far since that scary night when thirty-two of our brothers and sisters in Christ (plus hundreds more in a prayer chain) surrounded us and prayed for us. It was powerful. If you ask anyone who was there that night, they will tell you—something supernatural was going on. It was surreal.

Supernatural means something attributed to some force beyond scientific understanding or the laws of nature. It was God. It was prayer. It was love. As I look back, I can see the depth of our heavenly Father's love. He rearranged the universe that night to work everything that happened for our good and His glory. Going back to that night and remembering the apostle Paul's words helped me look forward to another three weeks.

> We can rejoice, too, when we run into problems and trials, for we know that they help us develop endurance. And endurance develops strength of character, and character strengthens our confident hope of salvation. (Romans 5:3–4 NLT)

We would get through.

Wednesday morning became a day of reflection. "It was the best of times. It was the worst of times." I've borrowed those words, but they do describe that period of our lives. This will sound strange, but I never felt like our experience with Isaiah's brain bleed was the worst thing that could happen. It had turned our lives upside down, but God's grace seemed to cover every part of it. Could it be that the power of prayer had masked the nightmare that was my life? I thought back to the only time I did feel as though I were in a nightmare—the night of September 8. But God had heard my prayer and the prayers of the thirty-two other people standing with Ozzy and me in that room. He heard the prayers of our church youth group after Charlie sent out a message telling them to stop whatever they were doing and pray. He heard every one of us, and He changed His mind. I don't know that I can explain what that truly means, but I know that's what happened.

From the moment I felt and knew God would save Isaiah, I could see blessings over the entire situation. From that time on, I never felt like it was the worst thing that could happen. We continued to see blessing after blessing every single day throughout the whole ordeal. Though challenging, they were some of the best times I ever had. Seeing God's grace, mercy, and overall awesomeness each day was incredible.

Having processed God's providence for us, I went back to focusing on the day ahead. Ozzy had taken the day off work, which meant I could do the same. I was gone most of Wednesday, spending time with friends who provided a fresh change of scenery.

When I returned to the hospital, Ozzy reported that Isaiah had wiggled the toes on his right foot. He also walked the length of the parallel bars with Shawn's assistance. I was thrilled for him but disappointed I missed it. He was still making progress in speech therapy and saying new words every day. His baby sister soon became a part of Isaiah's vocabulary as he began calling his pillow "Olivia." Sometimes the TV remote was a "remote," but sometimes it was a "bathroom." My brother Anthony called it "a game of one-armed charades" that gave me great satisfaction when I finally figured out what Isaiah was talking about.

After being away this time, I noticed that Isaiah was coping with my absence much better than the previous day. He had a great day with his dad, and he was happy. His confidence was building. It was a wonderful feeling.

> Consider it pure joy, my brothers and sisters, whenever you face trials of many kinds, because you know that the testing of your faith produces perseverance. Let perseverance finish its work so that you may be mature and complete, not lacking anything. (James 1:2–4)

It truly did feel like the best of times. I continued to be cautiously optimistic. Things were going well, but I wasn't naïve. I knew God could still allow challenges to come. I became increasingly concerned about how Isaiah's medications affected him and prayed God would give me direction on how to deal with that.

CHAPTER 11

THE GREAT PHYSICIAN

Thursday went well. For the first time, I got Isaiah up, showered, and dressed all by myself. What's interesting is that the showering didn't take as long as it usually did with the nurse assistants, and he was much calmer than any previous day. He handled the indignity well, but it had to be hard for a thirteen-year-old boy to be managed by a different stranger every day.

I was thrilled to witness him walking with assistance between the parallel bars. He walked back and forth about four times, which was twice what he did the previous day. Shawn was impressed with him and his work ethic. He worked hard, and I adored the look of joy on his face as he accomplished something new each day. I could see God's hand at work.

OT was a joy for me to watch as well. Isaiah was always the most entertaining during that time because Reagan allowed him or me to choose the music for part of his therapy. He would do his exercises to the rhythm of whatever song was playing, making it way more fun. Of course, OT today ended with him dancing to "Watch Me." I loved every minute of it.

He was equally impressive during speech therapy. He identified several more words than he had the day before, and he didn't watch the clock at all. He didn't even leave Carey a scented gift before I wheeled him out. So very thoughtful of him.

Wednesday evening, the night before, after talking to a friend who had been on the same anti-seizure medication Isaiah was on, I had decided to ask Dr. Soberon to take him off. My friend had mentioned how it made her a bit foggy sometimes. Her words were a revelation. A feeling in my spirit had told me that this medication was causing more problems than it was helping. Dr. Soberon wasn't there Thursday, but Dr. Kelley, filling in for her, was excellent. She told me if I didn't want Isaiah to take it, he didn't have to. She totally understood. In fact, she agreed with my assessment that the medication might be causing other problems in him.

I wonder how many times doctors prescribe drugs that even they don't even have confidence in. I certainly didn't have a good feeling about it. I believed it was affecting Isaiah's personality. I noticed the effect, especially when he woke up hungry. It was ugly. If I didn't give him something to eat right away, he would get agitated and upset. I thought back to that morning—he had thrown a tantrum because he had to wait twenty-five minutes for breakfast. Also, if the medication was suppressing something in his brain to prevent seizures, it seemed logical to me that it was suppressing other parts of the brain as well. He had never experienced a seizure, so it was prescribed only as a precaution. I felt that God, the Great Physician, had any possible risk covered, and that gave me peace concerning taking Isaiah off that medication. My God is bigger than whatever may come.

Dr. Soberon had also prescribed a medication to prevent muscle spasms. I didn't have a good feeling about that one either, and I planned to talk about it with her the next day. However, when the nurse came around to give Isaiah his medication, she told him what she was about to give him—as she always did—and he told her he didn't want it. I didn't hear their whole conversation because I had been talking to Ozzy on the phone.

When I hung up, the nurse stood there waiting for me. She looked a bit perplexed. "He told me he doesn't want it."

I smiled. "Well, don't give it to him then."

She said that if it were all right with me, then it was fine. It was all right with me.

When she walked out, I looked at Isaiah with a big grin on my face and asked him why he didn't want to take the medicine.

He pointed to himself. "I strong."

I almost lost it. "You don't think you need it?"

He smiled. "No, I strong."

"Did God tell you that you didn't need it?"

He nodded his head.

I leaned over and gave him a big hug. "Okay then. No more medicine." I had a massive grin on my face. "Isaiah, who told you that you're strong?"

"Me."

I love that kid.

He had never turned down what the nurses offered him before. He always unquestioningly took whatever they gave him. I am convinced God gave him the overwhelming sense he shouldn't "buy what they were selling" and he should reject the meds that day. I could see foregoing the anti-seizure medication that day had already made a difference in his brain functions. It had been more than twenty-four hours since he had taken the last dose, and he seemed more like his usual joyful self than he had in a while.

That day, Thursday, he communicated more than ever. When he tried to whistle along with a song, he couldn't. He became quite agitated but was able to say, "I can't whistle." It seemed a bigger deal than his inability to move his right side. When I gave him my dinner that night, he said, "Is this for me? Thank you!" My friend Amy came to visit, and when she hugged him, he said, "You smell good." When he felt sad around bedtime, he said, "Will you be in bed with me?" Of course, I did. After I positioned myself next to him in his bed, he said, "I miss home." That last statement brought tears to my eyes. I asked him if he wanted anything from home to make him comfortable. All he wanted was his own bedding. He also missed school.

What kid ever says they miss school? I guess one who doesn't have the option of going. His sadness was breaking my heart. "Is there anyone from school you want to see?"

He had hopeful eyes. "Mr. Kilgus."

Anyone who knows this man will understand. He was Isaiah's band director and a big part of why Isaiah loved to play the trumpet. He loved and encouraged Isaiah, and Isaiah loved him in return. I planned to work on Isaiah's wish list the next day.

I was learning to trust the Great Physician. Sometimes we get feelings about things. Those feelings are often God trying to tell us something, and it's key that we pay attention. Isaiah confirmed for me that day that I had heard what I thought I heard and that I could trust God with his recovery. Maybe this is the message God gave Isaiah that day: "Then your light will break forth like the dawn, and your healing will quickly appear; then your righteousness will go before you, and the glory of the Lord will be your rear guard" (Isaiah 58:8). It sure seemed so.

We slept in some again on Friday, which of course, was lovely. Getting up and starting each day had become more challenging as reality continued to set in. Isaiah found being away from home increasingly difficult, and I found it harder to pretend our days were some kind of mother and son weekend adventure.

The day started with speech therapy, and he did great until he found himself stuck on the word *bathroom*. He would try to say a word, and only "bathroom" would come out. We could see the frustration on his face, and then he said he felt dizzy. I jumped up and reclined the back of his wheelchair while Carey found a cool washcloth. His eyes welled up with tears, beads of sweat appeared on his face, and fear settled in his eyes. He started to pray out loud, saying, "God, please don't let this happen."

I wasn't sure my heart would be intact after this whole hospital ordeal. Carey and I encouraged him and let him know he would be okay. After a few minutes, he took the washcloth off his face, sat up, and said, "Okay," and was ready to get back to work. I think it was a panic attack of some kind. It made me realize that we might have to deal with some recurring fear in the future. I understood. It must be scary to be a thirteen-year-old kid, going about his day as usual, then waking up in the hospital days later with a tube down his throat. How could he be sure it wouldn't happen again? It shouldn't have happened in the first place.

We left Carey's office and headed toward the OT room. He started crying. "I miss home."

I took him to a corner of the OT room, put my arms around him, and let him cry. I didn't say anything. I did my best to remain strong for him. That may have been one of the saddest moments for me during our stay. Once again, all I could do was petition the Great Physician, begging him to heal Isaiah and let us go home.

It appeared the fog of the anti-seizure medicine had lifted, and his situation had become much clearer to him. Although this was a good thing, I could see that processing where he was and why would bring up many emotions. I realized then that he hadn't necessarily been handling the whole brain injury and hospital stay thing so well but that he may not have fully comprehended the severity of the situation.

Reagan gave Isaiah time to get himself together. She was sensitive to his emotions and didn't push him too hard. In his first session, all he had to do was sit in his chair with the electrode machine stimulating the muscles in his hand. Being the drama king he can be, he acted as if it were electrocuting him, so I turned on some inspirational music to distract him. Music saved the day once again. After all his therapies, we retired to our "suite" and took a good nap.

We had another slow start Saturday morning, not because we were lazy but because Isaiah was out of sorts. He ate breakfast, went to the bathroom, and then felt dizzy. A few minutes later, he felt worse. He put his blanket over his head because every ounce of light bothered him. His head hurt, and he felt nauseous. I called for the nurse to bring him some ibuprofen. He took it, but his head pain never improved. She told him that if he threw up, he needed to let someone know right away because they would get a CT scan. Well, he didn't throw up, but his headache did get worse. We let the nurse know. Dr. Kelley came in and said they were ordering a CT scan "stat." I knew the situation was serious, but I couldn't help but chuckle because I had just heard a real doctor say *stat*. Obviously, I had been in that place far too long.

Ozzy arrived right at that point. I had made plans earlier in the week to go with Olivia and our friend Sarah and her daughter Charlie to an American Girl doll fundraiser for the Butterfly Ministry for Girls. I felt torn for a split second about leaving in the middle of a crisis, and then I felt resolve. Ozzy was there. My girls were at home waiting for me, and I had to go.

A crazy thought went through my head. *What if Isaiah has another brain bleed and dies while I'm gone?* Well, I reasoned, if something happened while I was gone, I had spent the last twenty-six days loving that boy the best I could. I had told him so a minimum of ten times per day. I knew I wasn't in control. I couldn't stay and wait for the test results while missing precious time with my other children. I kissed him goodbye, told him I loved him, and walked out the door with perfect peace.

I stepped inside our house for only the second time since September 8—the first time being a quick visit to shower, change, and spend time with friends. I kissed and hugged my beautiful girls, took a shower, put on some fresh clothes, fussed at them for taking too long to get dressed, then ran out the door. It was so nice to hug those girls inside our house. I picked up Sarah and Charlie and left Abrianna with the rest of Sarah's family; then the four of us headed out to our event. We had a lovely afternoon. After the event, I left Olivia at Sarah's house with the rest of the crew, then drove back to the hospital.

When I stepped back into our room, Isaiah's face lit up, and he said, "Mom, I miss you." He gave me a huge hug and kiss, rubbed my face, and said, "You're soft." He looked at Ozzy and said, "Dad, she's soft." I guess he appreciated my softness after getting hugs from his dad and his six o'clock shadow all day. Ozzy proceeded to tell me how Isaiah had walked *by himself* on the parallel bars. I had missed it—again. Isaiah was beaming. He couldn't stop smiling. He was in the best mood he had been in since our time there. He was even giddy. He was also talking a *lot*.

With a big smile on his face and excitement in his voice, he said, "I can talk. I can sing."

He still wasn't one hundred percent, but what a difference another day had made. I couldn't help but think it had been the medicine holding him back. He spent the next thirty minutes or so listening to music and singing his little heart out. He was feeling like a real boy.

Do you ever wonder if your faith on any given day is just a fluke? As in, you were just in a good mood or something that day you trusted God? That day I found out that I still really did trust God. I know it sounds strange, but I am still surprised by my faith—that it is real and that I am living it out. I am thankful God continues to give me opportunities to trust Him daily. I have times of doubt, but during that period, those times were only moments. And in those moments, I would go back to the night it all began, when God showed me in a big way that it was okay to trust Him with my life—and with my son's life.

Like the psalmist, I wanted these words to be ones I lived by:

Let the morning bring me word of your unfailing love,
for I have put my trust in you.
Show me the way I should go,
for to you I entrust my life. (Psalm 143:8)

I had established that God had indeed changed His mind about taking Isaiah early, but what more would the Lord show us? For that, we would just have to wait in anticipation.

CHAPTER 12

JOY IN HOPE

Sunday, Isaiah and I were able to sleep on and off until close to noon. That never happened, but we deserved it. We had worked hard all week. Isaiah started the day with a shower, where a wonderful thing happened. Without any help, he lifted his right arm high enough to wash under it by himself. He laughed out loud the whole time he struggled to lift it. I joined him in laughter, as it was by far the most wonderful and exciting thing that would happen all day. We now find so much joy in things we used to take for granted. It was a blessing and delight, simply for him to lift an arm.

We thought it would be a quiet day because of the rainy weather, but Isaiah had many visitors. He was thrilled to see his band director, Mr. Kilgus, who visited with him for a while. Mr. Kilgus was visibly emotional when he saw Isaiah but handled it well. It was also a great day for Isaiah to see some friends from school he hadn't seen in a while. They all talked about how different school was without him there. He never knew before then what an impact he made on so many. I am thankful Ozzy and I have the kind of kid people miss when he's gone.

He ended the day visiting with a couple of other friends and his sisters, then played UNO with Isaac and Isabella, who are like family. Peace and contentment were all over his face. I noticed he had been embarrassed to speak much around the other visitors, but he felt comfortable trying on this night even if his speech wasn't perfect. Isaac and Isabella's dad, Will, who had survived a stroke a few years before, gave Isaiah some helpful advice. It was nice for him to talk with someone who knew what it felt like to be trapped inside his own head. He talked so much more now, but he still struggled to get words he saw in his mind out of his mouth. I could imagine how frustrating that would be.

That night as I was going to sleep, I looked back on my day with Isaiah and felt so much joy. I felt blessed to grow closer to Isaiah as we spent time together. I was not happy about the circumstances. I was not happy he had to struggle. I was not happy he was displaced from his home. I was not happy he couldn't play his trumpet. I was not happy he couldn't be out on the football field every day with his teammates. I was not happy he couldn't hug me with both arms. I was not happy, but still, I had a great deal of joy.

I could find joy because when he struggled, he appreciated his triumphs so much more. I could find joy because when his sisters were there with him, he was home. I could find joy because he still sang his favorite songs and made music in his heart. I could find joy because although he couldn't be with them physically, his teammates carried him in their hearts onto that field every single day. I could find joy because he was able to take one arm and hug me with the strength of two.

I know that through those trials, Isaiah learned things about life some people never will. He gained a level of wisdom some will never reach. He now understands the difference between the feeling of being happy and the depth of finding joy: "Surely you have granted him unending blessings and made him glad with the joy of your presence" (Psalm 21:6)

Webster says endurance is the "ability or strength to continue or last, especially despite fatigue, stress, or other adverse conditions; stamina." Isaiah and I were increasing our endurance daily. The joy we sought each day was part of enduring until we made it to the next one and the one after that. That Saturday we felt ready to go home but were content. Isaiah (and I) knew the situation could be much worse.

There were moments, though, when I thought he was losing himself—like that morning when he snapped at me while I tried to help him with his breakfast. I stopped what I was doing, looked at him, and then walked back to my area of our room. I refused to get upset or fight with him. He stared at me for a minute, recognizing that he may have hurt my feelings. He then said sorry several times.

It wasn't easy, but we did the best we could. I may have started to crumble at one point, however, because I found myself acting like a thirteen-year-old boy trying to outgas him. I know that's neither ladylike nor mom-like, but it was my truth. I felt sorry for anyone who came for a visit and walked into our room after a "battle."

All therapies continued to go well. Isaiah remained joyful about all he could do. Wow. His speech had significantly improved, and he hadn't used the word *when* in a few days. That morning, Carey and I decided he may have tapped into a part of his brain that generates telepathy. He randomly said, "Seventeen," right after she wrote it down on the paper in front of her. He didn't see what she had written but felt compelled to say seventeen. It was straight out of the *Twilight Zone*.

The date was October 5, and it was my dad's birthday. Before we had a chance to call him, he had already called to ask me a question. When I saw it was him, I handed the phone to Isaiah and told him to tell Papa "Happy Birthday." Isaiah answered the phone and then sang the whole "Happy Birthday" song, complete with cha-cha-chas. Needless to say, there were tears on the other end. Dad said it was the best birthday present he received that year.

We met with Dr. Cozbi, the neuropsychologist, that afternoon, and I found myself getting frustrated. She tried to tell me that Isaiah would experience depression, among other things, and she wanted him to take an antidepressant. I understand that many people, after going through what he had gone through, may deal with that. But Isaiah had continued to exhibit a supernatural joy, and it didn't look like that would change anytime soon. Depression was also not something he had ever struggled with before.

I understood it could happen, and I knew how to look out for any signs of it. It was already part of the prayers of many thousands who kept Isaiah lifted and wrapped in the arms of a loving God because we understand that depression affects many of God's faithful people. So if it appeared, we would deal with it at that time. But Isaiah continued to be more upset about his inability to whistle than he was about the inability to move his right side. He would be fine. He liked Dr. Cozbi a lot, so that was good. He wouldn't be telling her to go away like he did another doctor we knew.

After visiting with Dr. Cozbi, Isaiah wanted to get outside before he had company. We had heard the sun was out. My dad showed up right on time to join us, so we went together to the healing garden to soak it in. Unfortunately, by the time we made our way out there, clouds covered most of the sky. But it was still beautiful. Isaiah looked so relaxed. We sat for a while, and then I asked him if he had any thoughts.

He closed his eyes. "*Shh.*"

So I whispered, "Do you have any thoughts?"

He didn't answer. He sat there with his eyes closed, breathing deeply. After a minute, he opened his eyes and said, "Let's go!"

We went back inside, hit up Starbucks, then went back to our room.

Isaiah had a great visit with his friend Hayden, who brought him a Nerf basketball goal.

They had a blast playing together. Isaiah did well, making shots from his bed, and seemed to be embracing his left-handed status. Thank God for friends and family who did their best to help make his time there bearable. Our situation was not ideal, but we knew it wouldn't last forever. It felt like a marathon, but we had the best support providing us with refreshment and the emotional nourishment we needed to finish the race. Our job was to "be joyful in hope, patient in affliction, faithful in prayer" (Romans 12:12).

That night, as I thought back on the day, I smiled remembering Dr. Kelley's morning visit. She recognized the verbal progress Isaiah had made in such a short period of time and said I deserved an honorary MD for realizing that Isaiah should come off the anti-seizure and anti-muscle spasm medications. She said that she agreed with my decision. I took my "degree," not forgetting who it was who had educated me through faith; I knew that the actual MD belonged to our Creator. I decided to use its seal with confidence as I continued to make decisions for our boy.

I'm glad she thought me worth keeping on Isaiah's team because the next day, a certain someone would express quite clearly that it was time for me to go.

CHAPTER 13

TIME FOR MOM TO GO
(FIND REST)

Isaiah had a full schedule Tuesday, and he was eager to tackle it. What I didn't know was that he had his own plans for me. He rushed me along, making sure I had him fully dressed and in his chair ready for OT ten minutes early. It was an unusual Tuesday. I sent him to therapy by himself because I wanted him to know he could do it without me. When I told him he was going without me, a look of fear came over his face. I told him he would be fine and that he didn't need me.

He pleaded, "I do need you."

"You can still do it without me."

It clearly wasn't his first choice, but he did it. Afterward, he started his first session of recreational therapy (RT), and we both enjoyed it. We played a mean game of air hockey. I, of course, kicked his butt. To make it fair, I used my left hand. I decided to send Isaiah to his second PT session as well as the first part of speech therapy by himself. I joined him halfway through the latter and sat there for about ten minutes before he told me it was time to go. *Time for me to go?* Through the series of words he spoke, I figured out he was trying to focus, and I was distracting him. I told him that was just fine, and I would go back to our room and take a nap.

He did not hurt my feelings one bit. He had realized he could do it on his own. I was so proud. Hodding Carter said, "There are two gifts we must give our children. The one is roots. The other is wings." It seemed Isaiah was putting on his own wings, and I let him.

When he came back to our room with Carey, he told me he was sorry. I told him there was absolutely no reason to apologize because he finally knew he could do his work independently. He smiled, nodding his head in agreement. That was the last time I attended speech therapy with him.

During the day, Christine, the case manager, came to our room to let me know that the team of therapists had met to discuss Isaiah. They decided Isaiah would indeed be discharged in two weeks—on October 22—which included the extra week I had previously lamented over. I had mixed feelings about the decision. At that point, I was hoping they would add another week or two. Even though we wanted to go home, that hospital had become a safe place for Isaiah to recover. I wanted him to be truly ready to go home. Christine also informed me that RCP required us to have a ramp built to get inside our house before we could go home. That requirement cemented my resolve for Isaiah to be able to walk by the time we left. We did not want to have to make any significant changes to our house.

Isaiah and I had a great conversation about the possibilities. I told him Christine had given us a date to go home. He needed to work his behind off the next couple of weeks to show that team of therapists his God is bigger, and therefore, he would be able to walk out the RCP doors and walk up the steps into our house to lead a normal life. We talked about the fact that Shawn wanted him to go back on the medication that would reduce muscle spasms and help him walk better and faster. I explained to Isaiah that I would let him decide if that's what he wanted. He was the one who had to deal with spasms in his leg.

He gave me a look of determination. "No, I don't want it."

What he told me next about had me falling on the floor in the most dramatic fashion possible. He told me that God told him he didn't need it. I believed him. I knew that decision would bring about judgment, but that was okay. We were not going to do the drugs. I must admit, I felt a lot of frustration after talking to Shawn that day. I liked him, and I knew he wanted what was best for Isaiah, but I couldn't shake the faith that continued to grow throughout our journey. I had trusted God enough to approach His throne with the request of changing His mind. I continued to hold onto the Scriptures telling me what kind of God we serve.

I still found myself doubting Isaiah's ability to walk up the stairs of our house when the time came. That was the place I always seemed to find myself in when it came to trusting God. I would think, *I know He can, but will He?* Did He want Isaiah to walk up the stairs into our house, or was there another lesson to be learned by not accomplishing that feat quite yet? Should we have a ramp built just in case, or would he even need it? That's where I struggled.

Not long after Isaiah finished all of his therapies for the day, my dad came to visit. It was perfect timing because my friend Kendra had ended up in the ER with her son Gray, who was having some health problems. I was able to go to be with them. I went to support them, but I ended up having the best time laughing and clowning around with "framily," as Kendra likes to call friends who are like family. The wackiest friends were the ones who showed up first. Seriously. None of us are quite "right." It made for an interesting, awkward, and hilarious time in the ER with a teenager who feared the medical staff might have slipped some kind of drug into his IV fluids. Nope. It was his mom's goofy, middle-aged friends making him light-headed. I laughed so hard I cried, and when I left, I felt refreshed.

When I returned to our room, I found that Ozzy had come while I was gone and was enjoying the time hanging out with his son, showing him how to work out his abs so he could develop a six-pack. Isaiah spent some time staring at himself in the mirror and determined he had some work to do—guy stuff. He then gave me a serious look and told me I needed to go home.

What?

He said I needed to go home and sleep and that his dad could stay with him. I asked him if he was tired of me being in his face every day.

"No. Sorry I make you not sleep."

"Did someone tell you that you were keeping me from sleeping?"

"No." He pointed to his eyes and drew bags with his finger. "But only one."

I was only *allowed* to stay one night. That kid. I agreed to go home the next day, and I explained I was happy to be with him and he didn't have to be sorry. Many people had offered to stay with him, but I wanted to be the one. I continued to explain that where we were was not an ideal place to be together, but I genuinely enjoyed my time with him. Each day he surprised me and taught me something new. Although parts of his brain were impaired, other areas seemed to have been activated. He and I had become connected in a different way. He was E. T., and I was the pot of flowers.

Nevertheless, he permitted me to take a break and rest. And I looked forward to Wednesday night when I would get to sleep at home with my girls per Isaiah's orders. God was reminding me through Isaiah of the importance of rest. Even Jesus, though His activities were all good things, took time away to rest. Many places in the Bible show Jesus taking time off to refocus. In Mark 6:31, He invites His disciples to be with Him: "Then, because so many people were coming and going that they did not even have a chance to eat, he said to them, 'Come with me by yourselves to a quiet place and get some rest.'" I decided to do just that. I was determined to find a quiet place with Jesus and get some rest.

The following day, Isaiah showered and dressed 80 percent on his own. It was inspiring to watch. He pushed himself hard all day. He continued to ban me from all speech therapy sessions because I was a distraction. For some reason, however, he still felt he needed me for the other therapy sessions.

I did have the privilege of witnessing the strongest will I have ever seen in a person. During OT, Isaiah's leg started to shake. This shaking was the reason Dr. Soberon and Shawn wanted him to take the anti-muscle spasm medication. I pointed out that fact to him to make sure he understood what the drug was supposed to fix.

He understood. "I still don't want it."

I asked him if he planned to fix it himself. He agreed that was his plan.

I grew serious. "Okay. Then you're going to have to tell your brain to tell your leg to stop shaking."

He looked at me intensely. "Okay."

He looked so serious, I thought maybe he was upset, but then I realized he was in a zone, and he was talking to his brain. I wish I had a picture of what he was doing, but take my word for it—he was doing serious work. I believed he would succeed in healing his shake. There was something different about Isaiah. He had grown. He had matured. He was tapping into parts of his brain that were asleep for the first thirteen years and four months of his life. He had different eyes. He seemed to have a different connection with God as well. I'm not sure if I can accurately describe what I had seen and experienced in those several weeks in the hospital with Isaiah, but he knew something the rest of us didn't.

Ozzy came to the hospital right after work. As I was leaving our room to go home, I heard Ozzy say something about a DJ he had booked for the night and the fun they were going to have. I smiled and continued walking out the door. *Not my circus. Not my monkey. I'm going home.*

When I arrived home, I sat in the driveway for a minute and took a deep breath. I was already missing my boys. By the time I made it there, it was close to bedtime, and I wouldn't have much time with my girls, but it was nice to be under the same roof as them. I went into Olivia's room and crawled into bed with her. I asked her about her day and how her week had been so far. She was already falling asleep, so she had few words. I prayed with her, kissed her goodnight, then headed to Abrianna's room. She was ready for me. I climbed into her bed, and she snuggled up to me. As she laid her head on my shoulder, she exhaled a sigh of relief.

"I missed you, Mom."

"I missed you too, baby. Tell me what's been going on."

I listened as she caught me up on the latest high school news, including friends and teachers. I inhaled every precious moment.

When she finished, we prayed together, and then I went back to my room to reflect on the day.

One thing I knew for sure was that God was showing me His love through my children. The night before when Isaiah told me I had to go home, it was nothing but the Lord speaking through him. There was so much love in his eyes. There was so much understanding. I am beyond thankful to know God's love. It is astounding that He loves not only me but every one of us with a love we cannot fathom. As much as I love my son and daughters, God still loves them and me so much more than that.

What a blessing it is that I could almost feel his loving arms around me while my family and I went through this life-changing event. *That* is why I was okay. The grace you see in me is God's grace. The strength you think I have—it's His. The love you see in my eyes is God's love in me. It's real.

One of my all-time favorite Scriptures is Romans 8:37–38:

> No, in all these things we are more than conquerors through him who loved us. For I am convinced that neither death nor life, neither angels nor demons, neither the present nor the future, nor any powers, neither height nor depth, nor anything else in all creation, will be able to separate us from the love of God that is in Christ Jesus our Lord. Romans 8:37–38

As I continued to share the ins and outs of our days in the hospital through social media, it was difficult to accept all the nice things people were saying to and about me. It was all Jesus in me. I am not amazing—*He* is. I am not strong—*He* is. I am not special—*He* is. If I had traveled the journey on my own, you would have seen a hot mess. Any love seen in me was God's love.

That night, I was feeling thankful for motherhood and grateful for rest. I was thankful Isaiah had told me it was time to go. He was right. I stayed up for another couple of hours solely to enjoy the silence and alone time, then drifted peacefully off to sleep. Whatever would come the next day could take care of itself.

CHAPTER 14

FAMILY

Isaiah is a special kid—there's no doubt about that. But you should meet his sisters. They are amazing in their own ways, and I am proud to be their mom. They were both so patient through all our trials. Their world turned upside down, yet they still found joy and blessings in each day. They focused on their own tasks set before them and didn't allow our circumstances to overtake them. Some days were more challenging than others, but they handled them with grace.

When I returned to the hospital Thursday morning, I found Ozzy getting Isaiah ready for a shower. He didn't quite do it the way I did, but I was thankful he was doing it. I had to work on the ready judgment I often reserved for my husband, who will never do things the way I think he should but is always willing to serve his family however we need him. Ozzy is an amazing man and one of my biggest blessings. Isaiah is much like his dad.

Isaiah was in good spirits and asked both Ozzy and me for extra hugs. I think he was just so excited we were both with him that morning that he had to hug it out. That day he walked a total of ninety-six feet down the hall. The kid was determined. He said, "I strong," the whole way down the hall with every few steps. He was tired but refused to admit it, and he refused to quit. He kept that fighting spirit throughout the day.

Around dinner time, it was just the five of us hanging out together. It felt amazing. Being together meant more at that time than it ever had before. It was hard to watch Ozzy and the girls leave that evening, but we each did what we had to do.

Some things we could refrain from doing. Our children acquire habits and characteristics from us, and I won't share which parent Isaiah inherited his stubbornness from, but he gave me quite an exhibition that night.

Earlier in the day, Shawn had given Isaiah a special boot to wear on his right foot while sleeping. It would prevent his foot from pointing down and causing other problems with his leg. It was large and cumbersome, and I think it must have come to life that night and tried to murder Isaiah's leg because Isaiah had not been as upset about anything (aside from his staples being removed) as he was when I put that boot on him. There was crying and gnashing of teeth. The nurse, Karen, explained why he needed to wear it, but he made no attempt to listen to her. He wanted that thing off, and he was going to get it off or die trying. It became humorous as we watched Isaiah have a major meltdown. *Are you kidding me?* He said it was killing him, and he couldn't take it. I finally told him we could start with him wearing it for only one hour that night, and he reluctantly agreed.

I found one of his favorite shows to watch on Hulu to distract him from the boot, and I thought I could keep him absorbed enough that he would end up wearing it a little longer than an hour—but *no*. After precisely one hour had passed, he demanded the boot come off. Stinker. I pulled it off his leg, and he rolled over and went to sleep. Karen came in a few minutes after he fell asleep, and we looked at each other and burst out laughing. Oh, the drama of it all. Of all the things he had been through and fought through, it was going to be a boot that would take him out.

Before I went to sleep that night, I glanced around the room at dozens of cards, gifts, balloons, and treats. Isaiah was well loved, and all those things were an encouragement to both of us. I needed that reinforcement that night. *I think I can. I think I can. I think I can.*

During our time in the hospital, I became more aware of the importance of community. The way people embraced our family and met our needs inspired me to more proactively involve myself in other people's lives. We need each other. And we especially need that support when we're tired and unmotivated.

Hebrews 10:24–25 says it all:

> And let us consider how we may spur one another on toward love and good deeds, not giving up meeting together, as some are in the habit of doing, but encouraging one another—and all the more as you see the Day approaching. (Hebrews 10:24–25)

From the vantage point of that next morning, Friday, October 9, the two weeks ahead looked like two months. I was tired and needed motivation. Isaiah and I both started the day with heavy eyelids that never lightened throughout the day despite several naps. He said he didn't sleep well. Maybe I didn't either.

We ended the day again with the best people we could spend an evening with—family. I realized that in my prayers the few months previous to Isaiah's emergency event, I had asked God to draw our family closer to Him and closer to each other. I certainly didn't expect the method God chose, but that drawing together became one of the best parts of our journey. Our kids have always loved each other, but Isaiah and Olivia had butted heads during the last year, and all this was bringing the three of them a lot closer. The night before, on Thursday, Isaiah had even asked Olivia if she had homework due. He was concerned about her getting her work done. I expected that care to continue when we were living together again.

Earlier that day I found a text I had sent a friend on September 10, telling her I thought we'd be out of the hospital in a week or two. It never occurred to me then that Isaiah wouldn't be the same Isaiah he was two days before that. I thought maybe he would wake up and be back to his old self a week or two later. Boy, was I naïve. I thought a lot now about how different our lives would be soon. I wondered if I would still hold strong once we were home. I wondered if he'd have more frustrating days than he had in the hospital. I wondered if he would cry a lot. I wondered if I would cry a lot. I wondered if my emotions would resemble the ones I had when I brought my firstborn home more than fourteen years before.

I remember leaving the hospital with Abrianna and being excited to get home. The closer we came to our house, the quieter and more serious I became. I climbed out of the car with her in a carrier, feeling terrified to cross the threshold of the door. Reality had struck. I took my newborn baby upstairs to our room, then sat on the bed staring at her, unable to speak. I had to keep that tiny four-pound, four-ounce thing alive—for a long time. I finally collected myself, realizing that women had been keeping babies alive for centuries, and I could too.

The whole experience with Isaiah was much like taking care of a newborn baby, with each day bringing new lessons and challenges. The closer we came to going home, the quieter and more serious I grew. I wouldn't have a hospital staff to back me up when things became difficult. Ozzy and I had to keep that 179-pound boy alive—for a long time. I knew in my heart it would be fine. God was with me as he was when I first started on the path of parenthood. But man! Parenthood is no joke. It's hard. Throw an emergency brain surgery in the mix, and it's close to unbearable. Except it's not. I can do all things through Christ who strengthens me. So I could do anything. We could do it. *My* parents also continued their parenthood journey as they took care of my children and me. They had been taking care of our girls since that first night. I don't know where I would be without their love and sacrifice.

Actually, I do know where I'd be. I'd be in the mental health facility next door.

My mother, especially, sacrificed to fill in the gaps for our family. Psalm 20:2 says, "May he send you help from the sanctuary and grant you support from Zion." That's what God for did us. I knew that whatever struggles were waiting at home for us, the Lord would provide support to get us through.

Maybe it could start with someone helping me keep track of time. When I woke up the following morning, I didn't know what day it was.

Isaiah had different therapists on the weekends than during the week, so he had less enthusiasm for the therapists he didn't know as well—except for Whitney. He liked her. He knew her name but refused to call her Whitney. So when it was time to go, he would smirk and say, "Bye, Hanna." At least he doesn't call her Felicia.

Brent, who was visiting his wife, Linda, down the hall, came to pray with Isaiah shortly after lunch. He talked with Isaiah about the importance of praying specifically and fervently for what we need. So often, we pray for things as if they were a second thought. We mark Aunt So-and-so and those starving children in Africa off our checklist and move on. We often miss praying specifically for what we need. He prayed specifically for Isaiah's speech to be restored quickly so that he could tell his story. We believed God had a plan for Isaiah to tell of God's goodness through his struggles. I could hardly wait.

Later, we had the blessing of visiting with Ozzy's side of the family, who had come in from New York. Ozzy's dad, sister, and nephew drove down for the weekend. They came to the hospital along with Eddie, Sandee, and their three kids. The last time we had all been together was five years before in Hilton Head, the year before my mother-in-law passed away. I envisioned her smiling from heaven at the sight of all of us together again. I am thankful the visit was to see Isaiah in the hospital and not in a coffin. I am grateful to have married into a family I love and who loves my children and me. I am thankful we can celebrate life together.

After everyone left, Isaiah and I were each in our beds, and he looked at me and smiled.

I smiled back. "Are you happy it's just us again?"

He sighed. "Yes."

He'd had such a great day with friends and family, but he and I together had become our new normal and a place of comfort for both of us. The next day would be new, and he would forget how exhausted he was today. He would long to play UNO with his sisters and hug his dad's neck again.

And less than two weeks after that, we would have another new normal. I tried not to think too hard about it, but the closer we came to the day, the more anxious I felt. I knew God would be with me through it all. But at that point, all I had to focus on was Isaiah. When we went home, it would be *everything*. I had to breathe and recite Philippians 4:6. "Do not be anxious about anything, but in every situation, by prayer and petition, with thanksgiving, present [my] requests to God." I knew that wisdom, but sometimes I needed to be repeatedly reminded. That's okay. God understands. "And the peace of God, which transcends all understanding, will guard [my] heart and [my] mind in Christ Jesus" (Philippians 4:7). Amen.

CHAPTER 15

THE LORD IS GENEROUS

In Hebrew, the meaning of the name *Isaiah* is "the Lord is generous." This statement is always true, but our circumstances don't always make it clear. That season for us may have looked the opposite of a life full of God's generosity, yet I felt He had lavished us with the richest of blessings.

Maybe I was just becoming more aware of what God has always done. I think He may save each of our lives every day. Perhaps Isaiah had been close to death before that night—but I never knew. God is always good. We just don't always recognize His goodness.

That Sunday, we spent time with Scott and Deanne Ragin, a couple from church familiar with our rehabilitation facility. When they arrived, I was playing Connect Four with Isaiah. They bore witness to his amazing strategy as well as his unbelievable cheating skills. Four years previously, Scott had spent a month in rehab after having a stroke. He had been much worse off than Isaiah. It had been a dark and traumatizing time for their family. He told us he initially didn't think he would visit Isaiah because of the tough memories of his time at RCP. After a short while, though, he was glad he did. He found healing in the visit. We all warded off the tears over it, then ended up playing a long, uninterrupted game of Sorry. Isaiah played a cutthroat game, which made it kind of fun. (I'd never admit that to him. I'm striking out that sentence in any copy of this book he reads.)

Later, Isaiah's friends Collin and Zach came to visit. Before his hospital stay, Isaiah had been learning how to play the drums, so Collin brought a set of drumsticks to give Isaiah. He had wrapped them in blue tape and written "#coollikeisaiah" on them. I told Isaiah I was going to get a marker and add "#coollikeisaiah's mom" instead. He didn't think that was funny.

Sunday night, my friend Liz had a few women over to her home to celebrate our friend Michelle's birthday. Michelle was the friend who had reassured me Isaiah would be okay that night as we awaited his surgery. Isaiah gave me permission to leave and also to sleep at home. So I had a girl's night out, spent time with Abrianna and Olivia, and saw my in-laws again before they left to return to New York the following day. Blessings. That day was rich with blessings. Isaiah gave me a respite that showed me the generosity of our Creator.

I noticed the little things more than ever now. I had high hopes that the habit would stay long after this particular journey was over. I missed my husband. I probably needed to miss him. Maybe the experience would help us value any time we got to spend together more than we ever had before. Blessings. They are always there—sometimes we have to look a little closer.

Our God is a generous God. When I focus on all He has given me, it's difficult to see what I don't have. He's given me a beautiful family, a second chance at life with Isaiah, and daily gifts that I see more clearly now. Have you ever thought about gifts like flowers, trees, mountains, and sunsets? These are things we see every day but generally pay little attention to. He gave us those beautiful gifts for our pleasure alone. He didn't have to do that, but He is a generous Father who loves to give His children good things.

That night I slept *in my own bed*. But—it was the strangest thing—I had difficulty sleeping. When Isaiah told me to sleep at home, I wasn't excited. I guess I had become so accustomed to living in that little room, it had become somewhat comfortable. It felt like home. I don't think it's healthy to live as though a hospital room is home. Maybe I shouldn't have decorated so much. Perhaps the discomfort at my real home was the anxiety that continued to creep in when I thought about all that awaited us when we brought Isaiah home.

Why did those thoughts keep coming up? At least I was aware of it, so I took it to God, asking Him to calm my fears. I continually reminded myself that He would have it all worked out before we even arrived at the moment. He knew everything we were going to go through ahead of time and already had a plan in place to help us get through it. He had been faithful, and He wasn't going to stop anytime soon.

The next day was Monday, Columbus Day, and since Ozzy worked at a bank, he had the day off. First, I took the girls to school, then went back home and intended to do some chores around the house, but I was too tired. I took a morning nap, showered, and then left the house to get a few things I needed at the store. That's about all I could handle. I *had* to get back to the hospital.

Ozzy and Isaiah were napping when I returned. Isaiah's therapy sessions had gone well. Even though we saw improvement each day, the improvements were small. They weren't as obvious as they had been the first couple of weeks. Still, it was improvement.

I realized that we still needed to prepare for Isaiah being at less than 100 percent when he came home. We knew he could walk out of the hospital, but he also might need to sit right back down in a wheelchair. We were looking at the possibility of making changes to the house even though they might be temporary. I decided to be okay with it. Maybe these changes were still part of his journey—part of his story. After Ozzy woke up, he kissed me and Isaiah goodbye, then headed home, where he did all the things I had intended to do when I was there. I've got a good man.

After Isaiah finished his last therapy, he and I went to Starbucks. While sitting there, I realized he seemed much more present and aware than he had in previous weeks. I had been hesitant to share all that had been going on in my social media world because I wasn't sure how he would react. For a whole month, I had been sharing our journey on a Facebook page called "Pray for Isaiah." At the prompting of one of our PICU nurses, I had created it for close friends and family to update everyone all at once each day. It can be exhausting to tell the same story over and over each day. I would often read a touching message to him or let him see a few pictures, but only bits at a time. He was very emotional and would sometimes push my phone away because the emotion was too much for him. Our little page had drawn over two thousand followers. Most of them were strangers, and I shared almost all of Isaiah's journey with them. He had so many people sending him love and support each day, but I hadn't shared all of the posts and comments with him yet.

I pulled out my phone to show Isaiah a video of some kids in Honduras rooting for him. Our friend Jason was there and had told the kids all about Isaiah. Their words were precious, and Isaiah loved it. Then he started scrolling through the pictures and posts on the "Pray for Isaiah" page. He had never been interested in the whole page until that day.

My stomach fluttered because I didn't know how he would react to some of the thoughts I had put on the page. As he scrolled through, he stopped only to look at pictures and videos. He didn't seem too interested in reading what I had written—until he saw a picture of himself sitting in a wheelchair, covered in a blanket. He stopped there, where he read, "Today sucks."

Great. He had to stop at that one.

I watched him read, and as he did, my eyes welled up with tears. What if what he read made him sad? What if it angered him that I talked about him crying? He saw the number of people following his story. What if it was all too much for him to handle?

He read the whole thing, then said, "Wow."

I felt myself trembling. "Was that hard stuff, Isaiah?"

He wasn't looking at me. "Yes."

I knew he didn't remember anything, but I asked if he was okay with what I wrote and if maybe he was kind of glad I wrote it all out so we could go back and read about what happened during all those days.

He looked up at me. "Yes."

Whew! Okay. I did the right thing. No, I didn't ask his permission to write about him for that past month, but I felt compelled to do so. I could see he believed all of it meant something. His struggle meant something, and he understood that God was using it. We didn't allow him to read and see everything everyone had said or done for him because some of it was overwhelming. We gave him small doses at a time, but his eyes often brimmed with tears, and he would usually say something like, *Wow. Goodness. Wow. Whew.* It was big stuff. It was God stuff.

After Starbucks, we went outside to the healing garden with Papa, who had come while we were enjoying our drinks. They enjoyed some time together while I strolled to the opposite side of the garden and chatted on the phone with my sister, Victoria.

Isaiah had spent a lot of time over the weekend trying to remember how to say the names of his best friends. "Isaac, Isabella, Ian," he would say over and over. When he saw them again, he wanted to be able to say their names, and he did! He even sang "Happy Birthday" (Stevie Wonder style) for their mom, Michelle, whose birthday had been the day before. We were impressed. The night ended with his typical lift and release of offensive wind, a snack, a movie, and lots of laughter.

As much as I wanted to get back to a normal life, I would miss the time I spent with my son there at RCP, getting to know him in a way I never would have had he not had a life-threatening incident. I will cherish every excruciating and joy-filled moment. That night I rested in the knowledge that God knows each of us. He knows Isaiah. He prepared this life for us, and nothing can separate us from His love.

> Oh yes, you shaped me first inside, then out;
> you formed me in my mother's womb.
> I thank you, High God—you're breathtaking!
> Body and soul, I am marvelously made!
> I worship in adoration—what a creation!
> You know me inside and out,
> you know every bone in my body;
> You know exactly how I was made, bit by bit,
> how I was sculpted from nothing into something.
> Like an open book, you watched me grow from conception to birth;
> all the stages of my life were spread out before you,

The days of my life all prepared
before I'd even lived one day. (Psalm 139:13–16 MSG)

God continued His generosity through friends and family, through glimpses of Him amid trials, through the man I married, and so much more. Though I was blessed and grateful for my family and all God had given me, I still had a deep-seated fear that it wouldn't last.

CHAPTER 16

A FRESH START

It amazed me how much Isaiah had improved in a relatively short period. Just a few weeks before, I was doing flips because Isaiah smiled at me, then because he nodded or shook his head. Actions we had taken for granted for years became moments to celebrate—as we did when he was a baby. I've often compared our experience to having a newborn, but it occurred to me that September 8 may truly have been the day of Isaiah's "rebirth." It was as though God had hit the reset button on his life.

I could see things in Isaiah that were just as he was before, and then other things were new. He kept his great sense of humor and liked to show us how manly he was. He still loved to cuddle with his mom. He still loved to sing and listen to music.

But the new Isaiah desired control and order. He wanted things to happen on time and became anxious when they didn't. He brought all of us into his world of obsessive compulsivity. After outings, before he would get back in his bed, he would squint his eyes, looking intently across the sheets. The staff almost always changed his sheets while he was gone. He looked for the tiniest speck of lint or dirt on his bed and insisted that someone remove it. At one point, I joked I would name his story "The Prince and the Pea."

I wonder what it's like to be reborn as Isaiah had been. I imagine it could be painful. At the very least, it must be uncomfortable. I think that's probably how God intended it to be. When we go through changes, I think they need to be somewhat uncomfortable so we pay attention and recognize what's happening—or even recognize that God is doing *something*. What an extraordinary experience for Isaiah. He may not have seen the beauty in it at that point, but I could see it for him. God was changing him. He had a perfect design in mind and was taking time to sculpt Isaiah from the inside out. And when the new Isaiah emerges from his cocoon—oh my goodness! It's going to be something special. "Therefore if anyone is in Christ, the new creation has come: The old has gone, the new is here! (2 Corinthians 5:17).

—⁂—

As for me, it's possible I found a chink in my armor. For several days, I had experienced pain in my foot. I have a lot of issues with that foot anyway, so I usually take the pain and move along, but it grew increasingly bad. It felt as if I were endlessly stepping on a Lego on fire. The day before, I realized the problem was most likely plantar fasciitis. I didn't have time for it.

The pain made it increasingly difficult to do what I needed to do for Isaiah. That morning, I had less patience than I usually did when he refused to wear the hand splint Reagan had fashioned for him. It helped him keep his fingers straight out instead of curled up as they often were. Not wearing it would cause significant problems in the future. I had to be firm with him at five o'clock that morning when explaining why he had to wear it. Tears streamed down his face.

I was on the verge of my own tears. I had been asking God to heal my pain. I often experience guilt when asking Him to remove pain from my life. I know He doesn't want us to suffer from pain, but at the same time, I can't help but think of how Jesus suffered so much pain for each of us. The bit I was going through was nothing compared to what He endured:

> Surely he took up our pain and bore our suffering, yet we considered him punished by God, stricken by him, and afflicted. But he was pierced for our transgressions, he was crushed for our iniquities; the punishment that brought us peace was on him, and by his wounds we are healed. (Isaiah 53:4–5)

I can do this.

Isaiah had speech therapy, so I sent him off to wheel himself down the hall. I was pushing him to be more independent.

Five minutes after he left, Isaiah reappeared with Carey holding a tissue to his bloody nose. It was the third one he'd had since we'd been at RCP. I would usually pinch his nose and put ice on the back of his neck. This time, I grabbed a roll of toilet paper, put it under his nose, and pinched the bridge of it. This time, he insisted on blowing his nose. *Right.* I told him he could not do that because blowing would cause his nose to bleed even more. I usually let him blow gently once his nose had stopped actively bleeding to get the clot out, but we weren't even close to that point yet.

He kept saying, "Trust me, Mom. Let me."

I insisted that he didn't want to do that, but he wouldn't listen. He was fixated on blowing. He continued to blow, which caused his nose to bleed profusely. Carey called in Isaiah's nurse, Grace, who then found some ice to put on the back of his neck. The three of us stood there telling him to stop blowing as he became more and more agitated and continued to blow. Blood ran out of his nose, down his mouth, and all over his shirt. It was all over him.

He was crying, blowing, bleeding, and insisting I trust him and let him do what he wanted. He even grabbed my hand away from him as he tried to get me to listen to his "reasoning."

I leaned down and looked directly into his eyes. "I am your mother, and you need to trust *me*. I have never steered you wrong or done anything to hurt you. Why won't you trust me?"

I couldn't understand why he wouldn't listen to me. Maybe it was a result of the brain injury. Whatever it was, I became infuriated. So, I did the only other thing I could think of. I called his dad.

"You need to talk to your son. He has a bloody nose and insists on blowing it. He has blood all over him. It's ridiculous! I don't know what his problem is, but you need to tell him to listen!"

I put the phone to Isaiah's ear, fully expected to hear yelling or at least some kind of fussing coming from the receiver. *Yeah, he's going to get it now. Now he'll listen.*

What I heard was, "Isaiah? Are you okay?"

Are you okay? No! Give it to him! Tell him you're going to spank him or something!

My sweet husband continued to speak to him in a calm, gentle voice, telling him everything would be okay and that he needed to listen to and trust his mom. I took the phone away from Isaiah's ear and put it on mine.

"Okay. Thank you. You were much nicer than me." I felt small.

I put the phone down and focused on Isaiah. "Please don't blow," I said. "I promise it will stop if you don't blow." He was finally calm and stopped fighting. It didn't take long after that for the bleeding to stop.

I looked at Carey and Grace. We were all wide-eyed and looked a little beat up. Isaiah, however, looked broken. He sat there in his chair, his face wet with blood and tears, and stared off into the distance. He didn't even flinch when I took a picture to share with his dad. I asked him if he was upset. He barely shook his head no. I asked him if he wanted to be alone to talk with me. Carey and Grace started walking out before he even answered.

Once again, I leaned in close to his face. "Isaiah, I love you, and I would never do anything to harm you. You can always trust me to do what I think is best for you. Do you want some time alone to cry?"

He nodded his head yes.

I put my arms around him and gave him a hug and a kiss. He sobbed. I held him for a few minutes, then walked into the bathroom to give him time alone. When I came back, he was calm.

He looked at me with humility and determination. "Change it."

"Change what?"

He waved his hands all around. "Change it."

"Change your bed? Change the room?"

"No."

I didn't know what he was talking about.

Then he said, "New start."

"Oh, you want a fresh start? You want to start over?"

He smiled. "Yes."

That's my boy! I hugged him and told him that I loved him and that I was so proud of him. Then I asked him if he had just talked to God. "Yes," he said. I don't doubt he did. Only God could turn such drama and trauma around so quickly.

I helped Isaiah change out of his bloody clothes into fresh ones, and he was ready to go. He had used up all his time for speech therapy, but we stopped by Carey's office, where he told her he was sorry. Later, he also apologized to Grace. *Who is this kid, and who are his parents?*

We moved on to OT. There was dancing. Was that the same boy who was having a tantrum only twenty minutes earlier? Once again, I saw God in this experience. How many times do we lose it and throw down in front of our God? He's shown us how He wants us to live in a way that is good for us and glorifies Him, but we think we know better. I know I have deliberately done the opposite of what I knew in my heart God wanted for me. Somehow I always seem to think it will turn out well. I am always wrong. As much I think it's going to hurt to do what He's telling me to do, the result always ends up hurting me so much more. Why don't I listen? God is always faithful.

Isaiah believed it was going to hurt him to wait before he blew his nose. Even though I had proved my faithfulness to him repeatedly, he still didn't trust me. *Oh my goodness. That was God speaking right to me through my son's drama.* The good news for me and you is that God always gives us a fresh start if we ask Him. He will always draw us back into His arms and show us how much He loves us. That's what Jesus died for. His bloodstains take the place of ours. We must stop fighting Him long enough to see, feel, and accept His love. We must trust that He knows what's best. I'm working to stop doubting what I know He is saying to me. I want to listen to Him. I want to stop fighting Him. I'm tired of being tear-strewn and bloody.

> Create in me a pure heart, O God, and renew a steadfast spirit within me. Do not cast me from your presence or take your Holy Spirit from me. Restore to me the joy of your salvation and grant me a willing spirit, to sustain me. (Psalm 51:10–12)

God continues to make himself known through this whole experience. If what has happened to Isaiah brings more attention to who our God is, then bring it. As uncomfortable as I often am through this journey, I welcome the chance to honor God through it.

My heart just skipped a beat.

It's okay. *I can do this.*

CHAPTER 17

WHAT'S NORMAL?

From the very beginning of this journey, starting when I knew Isaiah would live, I chose to believe God would heal him completely. I chose to believe he would get back all he had lost, and if he wanted, he would be back on the football field the following year. I believed he would. However, as the days and weeks went on, I began a process of acceptance that our new normal might not be anything we had seen before. Maybe God's healing would look different from anything we ever expected.

Isaiah's vocabulary increased every day. I often caught him practicing. What I usually heard was something like this:

"*Hi*, how are you?

"Hi, how *are* you?

"Hi, how are *you*?"

Speech improvement was his most important goal because he understood he needed it to tell people what God had done for him. He was ready.

I know I say a lot of nice things about Isaiah, and they are all true. But he was still a normal thirteen-year-old boy. He still tried to cheat when he played UNO. He still offended me with his gas and fanned it in my direction. He didn't always listen the first time. He had a bad attitude sometimes when I did or said something he didn't like, and whenever someone told him he looked good, he answered, "Yeah," although I reminded him every single time simply to say *thank you*. I share his faults here because I want it to be known that God wasn't taking a perfect kid and using him for His glory. He took a completely normal and imperfect thirteen-year-old boy and used him for His glory, the same way He's taken that kid's extremely flawed mom and used her for His glory. I am so thankful God meets us where we are, then walks us the rest of the way.

It was Friday, six days before our release date. Ozzy brought the girls to the hospital that evening, and we spent the time talking, playing games, and trying to live as normally as possible. As we inched closer to our departure, I wanted to plan how we would pull off the rest of our journey. But I couldn't possibly—I had no idea what it would look like. So I decided not to worry about the unknown. I chose to rest in the knowledge that God loves me and would handle whatever we needed as He walked beside me. I chose to rest in the knowledge that He would carry me on the days I couldn't walk anymore.

I had a "moment" during OT as I watched Isaiah struggle to move his right arm, bend down, grab a colored beanbag out of a basket full of them, and lift it and place it on the mat next to him. His arm looked exactly like an arcade claw game. Exactly. His arm was wobbly as he tried to control it. When his hand finally hovered over the basket of beanbags, he slowly opened up his hand to choose one. Once he chose, Reagan had to help him close his hand around it. Then it took the strength of the whole right side of his body to carry that beanbag. As his arm wobbled back up, he struggled to bend his elbow to clear the edge of the mat he was sitting on so he could drop the beanbag next to him.

At that moment, for the very first time, I began mourning over his loss. I choked back tears as I watched him struggle. I felt conviction over my sadness. All he felt was excitement over being able to do something he couldn't do the week before. He was so proud of himself. I was proud of him too.

But he could do that two months ago.

How could this kid find joy as he struggled? He never showed anger over his loss. He only felt pride every time he accomplished something new. He felt joy.

Later, as I thought back to that morning, I felt sad. My heart flip-flopped as two competing truths wrestled within me: Isaiah was gaining so much more than he had lost, but he was just so young to go through so much and learn those lessons. Although I had found joy in each day's triumphs too, I was in awe that with only his blink-of-an-eye amount of life experience, Isaiah could do the same. I thanked God for protecting him from the negative feelings he could experience and asked that He continue to protect Isaiah throughout his struggle.

I had always prayed that God would put a hedge of protection around my family and me. So why didn't he protect Isaiah from a bleeding brain?

He protected him from death.

So many times, we ask God for something without realizing that the answer to our request may look different from what we thought it would. I remained aware that our journey could have gone a whole other direction. From the beginning, when Isaiah came into this world, I subconsciously prepared for his death. That preparation may be what compelled me to ask for his protection every single night of his life. I continued to thank God for the hedge of protection He did put around Isaiah. I thanked God for Isaiah's life. I thanked God for the struggle that brought me closer to Him and allowed me to honor Him through it.

I was thankful, but I took a little time to face the sadness I felt for Isaiah that night. I knew it was okay and not unfaithful or ungrateful. Because how could I appreciate the happiness if I never felt sad? How could I recognize and enjoy the good things if I never experienced the bad or the difficult? I couldn't. So I remained thankful. I took a little more time to mourn, then turned my focus and embraced Isaiah's joy.

Romans 15:13 reminds us that one of the purposes of joy is hope: "May the God of hope fill you with all joy and peace as you trust in him, so that you may overflow with hope by the power of the Holy Spirit." As I wrapped my heart around Isaiah's joy, I strengthened my hold on the hope we would one day get back to normal—whatever that was.

The next day was Sunday, my favorite day of the week. I always looked forward to Sunday because it was truly our day of rest. No therapy and no hurry. In the morning, we prayed and did a devotional together. I loved listening to Isaiah pray. It was still mostly *thank you*. Shouldn't those words be the most significant portion of *our* prayers too?

I asked him if he was going to miss that place, and he quickly answered no. I asked him if he would miss our time together, and he quickly answered yes. We still had a ways to go before our exclusive time together ended, even after going home, but I was glad to know he cherished it as much as I did.

We enjoyed time with Jim and Lori Maxey from church, who brought us communion, then continued a Harry Potter marathon we had begun before they came. After a while, I told Isaiah we needed to get out. So we bought our drinks and our pumpkin cheesecake muffins, then headed to our regular date spot—the Healing Garden. Yeah, it was our new normal. For a moment, I felt I could keep this normal forever. It was such a beautiful, crisp fall day. The air smelled clean and even had a hint of an unknown flower. Isaiah smiled and took a deep breath as soon as we went through the doors that opened up to the garden. We hung out there for a while, enjoying the fresh air and using my phone to look through old pictures on Facebook. We found photos of the first time Isaiah served communion, the first time he prayed over communion, and the first time he gave a sermon. He started serving the Lord at a young age.

I became incredibly grateful for those days of rest. They allowed both of us to reboot and prepare for the week ahead. I even had time to think about the importance of rest and renewal. The first four verses of Psalm 23 came to mind.

> The Lord is my shepherd, I lack nothing.
> He makes me lie down in green pastures,
> he leads me beside quiet waters,
> he refreshes my soul.
> He guides me along the right paths
> for his name's sake.

Even though I walk
through the darkest valley,
I will fear no evil,
for you are with me;
your rod and your staff,
they comfort me. (vv. 23:1–4)

People who don't believe in God might call me a "sheep"—and not in a good way—but because I'm a Christian and because sheep "just follow." Well, I am not just any follower, and my shepherd is no ordinary shepherd. A shepherd cares for his sheep by meeting all their needs, guiding them, and protecting them. When sheep wander off, they are in danger of getting lost, attacked, or falling off a cliff. He uses his rod as a weapon to keep evil away. He also guides the sheep with his staff to places where they can rest and renew before continuing their journey. He guides them to safe places. We *are* like sheep. We *do* need guidance and protection. So we'd all better follow a good shepherd.

My shepherd cares for me. When I am in a dark valley, I don't have to worry. He comforts me every time (a kind word from a stranger or God-sent peace). He leads me to places of quiet rest (like this healing garden). He meets all my needs (all these friends who have cleaned my house, fed my family and me, and countless other kindnesses). Sometimes I experience supernatural interventions, and sometimes He simply works through others. However He chooses to work in me, I will continue to follow my Good Shepherd.

There are times when I continue to go and go and wouldn't stop if He didn't stop me. There are times He makes me rest because I don't always have enough sense to do it on my own. Sometimes He speaks through my son, who tells me it's time to sleep. He refreshes my soul.

That Sunday, my simple refreshment came in the form of Isaiah's sweet face as we waited in line at Starbucks. He gave me a genuine smile, and right then and there, my soul was refreshed.

I'll take all the refreshment I can get before the next challenge rears its ugly head. We might have rested in our new normal today, but change was coming.

CHAPTER 18

PREPARING FOR HOME

saiah went up and down the stairs during PT. It was an incredible sight. He was working harder than ever as we neared the end of our stay. He continued to do things he couldn't do days before. I was astonished.

I was excited to celebrate Isaiah and had asked him a couple of days before if he wanted lots of people outside cheering him on as he left the hospital.

He scrunched up his face. "No. Family."

I asked him again today to see if anything had changed.

He looked worried. "But I can't talk."

In Isaiah's mind, he thought a crowd of people meant he had to give a speech. I assured him that no one would require a speech from him. But he still felt strongly about only his family being there. Honestly, I was hoping that's what he would say because I felt it would be too overwhelming to have more people than that.

I loved that he ascribed *crowds* to speaking. He was already preparing his heart and mind for what he felt God would call him to do one day. Even though being the Lord's mouthpiece wasn't an expectation at that point, I did remind him of the story of Moses. When God told Moses to go before Israel's elders—and eventually the king of Egypt—to give them a message, he told God that he wasn't a good speaker. God answered, "Who gave human beings their mouths? Who makes them deaf or mute? Who gives them sight or makes them blind? Is it not I, the Lord? Now go; I will help you speak and will teach you what to say" (Exodus 4:11–12). God is the same God today that He was then. He will give Isaiah the words when it's time.

God had a lesson for me that day as well. We had entered our sixth week of hospitalization, and as we approached the day of discharge, we continued to have our friends and community offer help for the near future. It's funny how I have no problem offering to help someone and fully expect they will let me, but I have such a hard time accepting help. It takes a humble heart to accept help. I think I'm a relatively humble person, but accepting help requires a different kind of humility.

I read that grace is, very simply, a gift. How discourteous it would be to reject God's gift of grace. Warren Wiersbe said, "You don't earn grace, and you don't deserve grace; you simply receive it as God's loving gift and then share it with others."[1] I guess I resemble that quote. I hardly presume I am deserving of that gift. So many others are more deserving than I am. I get it though. Deserving is not the point. It's a gift.

God often shows His grace through others. I have to look at this problem of mine that way. If someone chooses to give me a gift from their heart, wraps it up, and hands it to me, I should never reject it. That would be rude (even if I'm still uncomfortable with it). In this situation, that gift is—more than anything else—God's grace.

Having gone through this experience, I vowed I would be more mindful about sharing the gift of God's grace with others. Wouldn't we all be so much better off if we would just let go of the not-deserving part and simply accept God's grace and be thankful for it? The best gift of all was God sending His Son to live on earth as one of us and then sacrificing His life to save ours. He freely gave us that gift. Why do so many of us reject it? If God says we're worth it, then we are worth it. *You* are worth it. That night I celebrated the gift of peace. I celebrated the gift of compassion. I celebrated the gift of friendship. I celebrated the gift of loving generosity. I celebrated the gift of Christ

---

1   Warren Wiersbe and Jim Cymbala, *On Being a Servant of God*, revised ed (Baker Books, 2007).

that embodies every single one of those things. "Every good and perfect gift is from above, coming down from the Father of the heavenly lights, who does not change like shifting shadows" (James 1:17)

—⁓—

It was getting real.

I had an appointment that Tuesday, so I left Isaiah in the capable hands of my mom. She told me that during PT, Shawn showed her how to get Isaiah up off the floor if he fell. Isaiah said it was hard for him; he had to get down on the floor to teach her. I wanted to be confident we wouldn't have any falls because Isaiah would be extremely careful as he navigated his way through the house in his new condition. He proved to me that evening, however, how likely it was a fall would happen.

He was sitting on the side of the bed, which he often does when he's hot. I looked down for a minute, then heard him say, "Mom, help." I looked up and saw him sliding down toward the floor, with his left hand twisted slightly behind his back as he tried to push himself back up. Hospital beds are generally much higher than the average bed at home. I hurried over to him and was able to help him back up onto the bed.

I was aggravated. You know when your kid does something dangerous and gets hurt or almost hurt, and you want to wring their neck when you think about what could have happened? Yeah. I had one of those moments. I had to remind Isaiah every day not to get overconfident in his ability to stand, sit, or move from the bed to his wheelchair. I don't know what he was trying to do, but it was something he shouldn't have done.

I kept my cool and asked, "Do you understand now why I keep telling you to be careful and not to get overconfident about what you can do?"

He took a deep breath and nodded. "Yes." It had shaken him.

"That was scary, wasn't it?"

He nodded.

"Did you learn your lesson? Do you understand that you need to ask for help?"

Again, he nodded.

Of course, I had to continue with the obligatory "Mom rant."

"Do you know it could have been a lot worse, and you could have been hurt really bad? That is why you have to listen to me. That is why you have to trust me. I'm trying to keep you safe!"

One last nod and a deep breath.

Oh, that boy! The sad thing is that he had learned his lesson for that day, but the next day or the day after that, he would most likely push the limits again, forgetting what happened the day before. He'd be overconfident and start thinking he could do it regardless of what I told him.

He often thinks I might be wrong—that he can do anything without help.

That sentiment sounds familiar.

The experience was another lesson for me. Too many times in the recent past, I have tried to do things on my own without asking for God's help or guidance. Thank God I always get more chances to do it right—more opportunities to listen.

Proverbs 24:16 says, "For though the righteous fall seven times, they rise again." When I fall, I need to remember that God will always help me back up. I may have to experience a "God rant" through His Word, but at least I know He loves me and wants to keep me safe. Over the years, I've realized that in the Bible, every time God encourages or prohibits something, it is all about our safety or our health. I didn't understand this concept growing up. I thought God was just this super bossy being whom I had to obey because He was powerful and because He said so. As I grew older, I realized there were reasons behind His words. He cares for our physical, spiritual, and emotional health. Even if I don't understand why He tells me to do or not do something, I must remember that He sees what I am unable to see, so I need to trust Him completely and obey. He loves me and wants the best for me. You too.

How was it possible the next day would be our last full day at RCP Hospital? So much had happened there. So many experiences are etched forever into the walls of my heart and mind. But I knew that place was not the end of our story. A whole new chapter was coming— a new set of challenges laid before us. I was doing my best to listen to what God was saying to me. I prayed Isaiah was too.

"Trust in the Lord with all your heart and lean not on your own understanding; in all your ways submit to him, and he will make your paths straight" (Proverbs 3:5–6). I knew whatever road we were to travel next would be one I would need extra guidance on. I prayed I wouldn't get lost.

CHAPTER 19

JOY STOLEN

We had only one day before going home, and I let someone steal my joy.

Isaiah and I woke up psyched to begin our last full day in the hospital. Reagan came in first thing to help him with his shower and getting dressed and to evaluate his readiness for the last time before leaving RCP. He did great. He was ready for home. She brought him the special green shirt reserved for those who carry the distinguished title of graduate. He laughed as he looked in the mirror, agreeing that the color looked great on him. He had a grin on his face from the time he woke up through the end of the day.

PT consisted of getting ready to travel as well as accident preparation and prevention. Shawn taught me how to get Isaiah off the floor if he fell and how to transfer him to the car from his wheelchair. Isaiah was so pumped to sit in a car, even if only for a moment.

He had another session with Reagan where she showed me some exercises to do at home with him. Isaiah showed off new skills he seemed to have developed overnight. He could now isolate some finger movement in his right hand. He was immensely proud, and so were we. Of course, he ended the session the way he should—with the whip and nae nae.

Dr. Cozbi tested him as did Carey. Isaiah allowed me to sit in with him during his final speech therapy session as long as I promised to be silent. Carey asked him a ton of questions, and he did *so* well. It was awesome to see how far he had come since the first day.

That afternoon, my friend Kendra came for a visit, and while Isaiah was in therapy, she and I had a chance to visit in our room. About twenty minutes into our visit, Dr. Cozbi came in to talk about Isaiah's discharge the next day. I let her know she could speak freely in front of Kendra. She once again brought up giving Isaiah an antidepressant and even had a prescription in her hand along with other paperwork. She explained that it would not be for depression but to get the chemistry in his brain "right." *Oh good grief, woman.* There was no indication from any of the medical doctors that his brain chemistry was off. Based on how she tried to trick me with words, I concluded that she was unaware of my intelligence.

She proceeded to try every approach to get me to agree to what she wanted. "Mrs. Custodio, you need to trust those of us who know what we are doing medically for your son. Studies have shown that brain injury patients go through many mental and emotional changes and highly benefit from medication to combat depression or any other chemical imbalance."

My body tensed up even more than it already was. "He doesn't have depression. How many teenagers do you get in here?"

She looked annoyed. "Well, not many, but we have a certain protocol for our patients."

My eyes narrowed. "I'm guessing you almost never see them. You cannot treat a thirteen-year-old kid the same as you would an adult. Like I told you before, I know what to look for, and if I see any signs of depression, we can discuss medication then."

She shifted in the chair she was sitting in. "Mrs. Custodio, you are one of the most intelligent, involved, and wonderful parents we have ever seen. You have a great reputation with the staff here, and they have been very impressed."

Double good grief! I forced the corners of my mouth to move a bit upward. "Thanks. So you should understand that I am declining medication for my son."

She looked angry. "You need to think of the best interest of Isaiah. A good parent does what is best for their child, and you need to trust me when I tell you this is what he needs. I have been a neuropsychologist for a long time, and I know what he needs. You are not acting in Isaiah's best interest by refusing to give him these meds."

At that point, the anger that had started at my toes had worked its way up to my brain. *Did this woman just try to tell me in almost the same breath that I am a wonderful mother but a horrible mother too?* I stood up, which was her cue to get out. "We're done here. You are going to give me time to decide what we are going to do. You are not going to bully me into anything today."

She looked shocked and awkwardly said goodbye and hurried out of the room.

I was able to keep my cool, but I felt my head was going to explode. Thankfully—and I'm sure it was God-orchestrated—Kendra was there to witness it all. I almost thought I had imagined that the conversation had happened the way it did. I asked Kendra if she heard everything I had and if I were losing my mind or had Dr. Cozbi seriously played four different roles in one conversation. She validated my feelings and kept me grounded. It took me the whole rest of the day to stop being furious. What upset me even more was that I allowed that woman to upset me so much.

I was also grateful that I had scheduled to meet with Pam Childress, whom I had never met before. My friend Sarah had connected us as she felt Pam could prepare me for feelings I might face going home with a child who would never be the same. A couple of years before, her daughter had been shot near her college campus and is now paralyzed from the waist down. Pam came in when I was still hot with anger, which unsettled me. But I explained what had just happened, and she, too, validated my feelings and helped me not feel as though I were a crazy person. The wisdom she then shared extended beyond the going-home emotions to ones I might encounter even months and years later. Ours was a divine appointment at precisely the right time. She explained that Isaiah would likely be a very different person than he was before, and that I would need to be patient not only with him but also with myself.

Later, I was still thinking about that unnerving conversation with Dr. Cozbi. I decided to scribble my feelings down on a piece of paper, then promptly headed toward the offender's office. Thank God she wasn't there. I was not in a loving mindset at that time. God knew I needed time.

When I sent Kendra a text later about my struggle with anger, she reminded me not to allow that woman to steal my joy. How right she was. I was disappointed I allowed one person, who doesn't know or care for me, to steal the joy I started the day with. How could I let Satan creep in and do that to me?

I knew that's exactly who it was. "Be sober-minded; be watchful. Your adversary, the devil, prowls around like a roaring lion, seeking someone to devour" (1 Peter 5:8 ESV). I prayed and asked God to help me calm down. To help me let it go. To help me find my joy again. Even as I think back today, I still hold a twinge of anger toward that woman. I need to separate her words and actions from who she genuinely is. I've worked to see her as a child of God just as I am. I've had to, or the anger would eat me up inside.

A friend once told me that holding a grudge is like drinking poison and waiting for the other person to die. That's not who I ever want to be. I needed that Scripture again. "Create in me a clean heart, O God, and renew a right spirit within me" (Psalm 51:10 ESV).

I prayed God would help me change my frame of mind and put the whole exchange into perspective. He did provide another person to help me see the conversation differently and begin to let it go. I continued to pray until I found a place of peace. I'm so thankful I can do that with God. He understands when we face hurt or anger and can't seem to let something go. He gets it. God is that friend who sits and listens to us patiently over and over, allowing us to vent, until finally, He says, *Stop. That's enough. My grace is sufficient. Get over it.*

Yes, Lord. I hear you.

Once I worked through that problem—for the most part—I remembered that we were going home! That night, I kept looking at Isaiah with a big grin on my face and reminding him we were going home the next day.

While the night marked the end of that particular chapter of our journey, I knew that a new and maybe even more difficult one would begin the next day. I felt the upcoming weeks and months would test my faith even more than what we had been through during those first six weeks.

I was ready.

PART THREE

WHO'S IN CHARGE NOW?

CHAPTER 20

(NOT) ON OUR OWN

That final Thursday morning, I woke up before the sun and couldn't go back to sleep. It wasn't the excitement of going home that kept my eyes from closing. It was the near dread of leaving what I had grown so accustomed to for six weeks. I thought about having to say goodbye to all the therapists who had become a part of an extraordinary family of people responsible for shaping who Isaiah is and will be.

I cried.

I sat there in the dark and I cried. Then I started to get anxious because I didn't want to cry in front of those people, knowing it would be a cry of the ugly variety. By the time I collected myself, Isaiah was awake and ready to eat. He looked so handsome. His barber had made a special trip to the hospital the evening before to give him a nice haircut.

I stood up and put my nose to his nose. "Guess what day it is?"

He smiled big. "Home."

"Yes!" I didn't feel that excited for myself, but I did feel it for him.

We ate breakfast, and then I started packing. Ozzy and my dad came to help. It was like packing up a college dorm room. I took my time burning the images of every wall into my memory. Every poster, card, game, stuffed animal, basket of goodies, signed football, jersey, blanket—every piece of love—was removed from its temporary home and packed up. We said goodbye with hugs, gifts, and kind words— and a few tears—to all our therapists and nurses. I kept it together for the most part. Isaiah and I would miss seeing those faces every day.

Isaiah looked so grown up and handsome sitting in his wheel-chair with his fresh haircut, waiting to leave. He sat up taller than he had since we'd been there. He was a changed boy. When we finally said our goodbyes to everyone at RCP Rehabilitation Hospital, we headed downstairs, where Isaiah's surprise ride was waiting for him. I expected him to walk from the door to that ride, but he flew past us in his wheelchair and headed straight for the automatic doors. He didn't even wait to make sure they would open. They opened only seconds before he passed through.

Once he made it outside, he saw his papa's truck and stopped. Behind it was a limo. He noticed we were all staring at him in antici-pation. He pointed to himself and said, "For me?" We told him it was, and his mouth dropped open. If he could have jumped up and down, I'm sure he would have. His eyes grew wide. "Yes!" He looked as if he might levitate out of his wheelchair. He couldn't wait to get in.

Ozzy, Isaiah, and I climbed into the limo. We rode around to the other side of the building, to the Children's Hospital, and took a quick trip to the PICU to see the nurses who had taken care of him at the very beginning. Isaiah doesn't remember anything about the PICU, but as we made our way down the hallway, I explained that he was about to meet part of a team of people who had kept him alive at the beginning of his journey.

"Whoa" was all he said.

Exactly.

It was no coincidence that our two favorite nurses, Crystal and Clarissa, happened to be working that morning. God had orchestrated even that detail. They were thrilled to see Isaiah doing so well and getting to leave, and there were tears. We said goodbye, promised to visit, then went back to our limo and headed home. Though joy was rippling through me, it wasn't enough to calm the butterflies nervously dancing in my stomach. The feeling was quite familiar.

We pulled up to the house and opened the garage door. When the garage door went up, you would have thought a million dollars was piled inside. Isaiah gasped in amazement.

He laughed and laughed and said whoa and wow repeatedly. The ramp to the interior door looked like a Hot Wheels track. Some friends from church had lovingly built it to make it easier to get into the house. He loved it.

We went into the house, and that bringing-my-first-baby-home feeling showed up. Our sweet English setter, Blue, jumped around as he greeted us at the door. His wagging tail was like a whip, and Ozzy held him back so we didn't have any mishaps as we walked Isaiah from the garage door to the kitchen. Our cat Lola stood at the top of the stairs. She glanced down at us, then haughtily turned and found a corner somewhere upstairs to curl up in.

We had a tough moment after arriving when Isaiah had to go to the bathroom. Our bathroom was not made for wheelchairs—neither was the rest of the house. I wished we could pick up and move to make it easier for Isaiah, but I was sure this obstacle was part of the journey. I asked him how he felt about it, and he said, "It's hard." I let him know I understood, but the situation was only temporary. I had to remind myself of that as well. I knew he would have some sad moments, but that's what I dreaded most. Nobody wants to see their child sad or in pain.

We navigated through the rest of that Thursday relatively well. Isaiah became restless in the early evening and asked if the family could go for a walk. We pushed him through the neighborhood in his wheel-chair. It was a beautiful day. It would have been perfect, but we had to go without Abrianna. My mom had taken her to see a doctor about mysterious bumps that had appeared around her shoulder. They looked like chickenpox. The worst part was that she couldn't hug her brother when she finally came home, in case she had the pox. Thankfully, they simply turned out to be a strange form of eczema.

We enjoyed a delicious dinner delivered to us, and we sat down as a family to eat it. Together. It was a good—but also overwhelming and emotionally draining—day. I was grateful to end it by snuggling in bed with my firstborn and chatting for a while. We talked about

September 8 and all the other happenings in her life I needed to catch up on. I had missed her.

As I was walking out of her room, she said, "I'm glad we got to talk."

I felt blessed to have a teenage daughter who actually liked to talk to me and would still snuggle. I needed it as much as she did. Olivia was tired and had already fallen asleep as I prayed with her earlier but seemed relieved to have all of us back together again.

That first night back home, I had a hard time thinking about sleeping without Isaiah next to me. I wasn't sure I would be able to sleep. We had borrowed a video monitor from a friend and set it up on a nightstand. I found myself staring at the screen until my eyes crossed.

They say home is where the heart is, but I find that my heart is wherever my family is. It was nice to be home, but surprisingly, that structure held little sentiment for me. All the bedrooms were filled that night; therefore, my heart was present within each of them.

Our "newborn baby" was quite a challenge. I managed to doze off for a few minutes at a time, but every movement or noise coming from Isaiah's room through the monitor had me on edge. He called Ozzy or me at least five times during the night to go to the bathroom, and I had to get up a few other times because we heard and saw him sit up in the bed. My instinct was to say I didn't sign up for this, but I did. I absolutely did, and I didn't regret it.

Friday morning, Ozzy made breakfast, so I brought it to Isaiah and hoped he would go back to sleep after eating, but no such luck. I helped him walk to our room, helped him into our bed, handed him an iPad, and begged him to let me sleep more before we started our day. He agreed, and I dozed off and on. I slept much better with him sitting in the bed next to me. Abrianna had the day off from school, so I didn't need to get up for anyone else as far as I was concerned.

Close to lunchtime, after being so patient, Isaiah decided he'd had enough and said, "Mom. I don't want this. Have to work hard."

I laughed. "What? You don't want to lie in bed all day?"

"No. Have to work."

I started him with the exercises Reagan gave us because he could do them in our bed, which is about the size of the mat they use in therapy. He was totally on to me, though, because after a while he gave me a look and said, "Mom." *Okay!* I made him a sandwich, and we ate lunch at the kitchen table. At least we had kept with the hospital schedule of lunch at half-past eleven. I had almost forgotten that after lunch, I was supposed to go to a student-led parent-teacher conference at Abrianna's school scheduled for one o'clock. I moved quickly and changed out of my pajamas. My mom came over to stay with Isaiah, and Abrianna and I took off.

When we returned home, Isaiah was thrilled to inform me that he had discovered he could do squats on his own. He was one determined, hardworking kid.

We were trying to get into a rhythm of normalcy, though I had no idea what normal would mean. We'd been on our own only twenty-four hours, and I thought we were rocking it. Then this.

It was late afternoon, and Isaiah asked for a snack. We still had lots of snacks left over from the gift baskets he had received at the hospital. I found a blueberry-muffin-flavored Larabar. It had been a while since I'd had one, so all I remembered was that they contained a bunch of mashed-up fruit pressed together into a bar.

Right after Isaiah finished the bar, he wheeled himself to the bathroom. He had been drinking so much water since he came home that he headed to the bathroom every ten to twenty minutes for hours and had become skilled at navigating this challenging obstacle from our first day. He became so good at it that after a while I didn't have to stand right there with him. But when he was done this time and came out, he looked at me and pointed to his neck. "Mom. Feels bad." He had a funny look on his face like he had a bad taste in his mouth.

I asked him if he needed some water, and he shook his head no. I asked him what he needed.

He kept pointing to his neck and smacking his lips like he was trying to get rid of the bad taste. Then he said, "Cashews."

I gasped. "Oh no!" I ran to the trash can, pulled out the empty Larabar wrapper, and looked through the ingredients. There it was. Cashews. He is highly allergic to cashews. I called my friend Wendy, who has a lot of allergy experience, and asked what I should do. I didn't have any liquid Benadryl. Would the tablets work in time?

She told me the liquid is better. I yelled to Abrianna that I'd be right back, flew out the door to a neighbor's house, and asked if they had any liquid Benadryl. They did not, so I ran back home and grabbed the box of Benadryl. The instructions said to give children over twelve and adults between one and two tablets. I gave him three. I looked him over and noticed his eyes were a bit puffy. Wendy told me to check his tongue. I couldn't tell if it was swollen, but I could see that his taste buds were. He was breathing okay, but he said his chest felt tight. He was nervous. He knew it could be serious.

I kept Wendy on the phone for about thirty minutes while I watched him. The allergy reaction never escalated. He was okay. Here's the thing: Isaiah had had an allergic reaction to cashews only one time before. That was the first and last time he ever ate a cashew. Since we found out he was allergic, we had been diligent about keeping him away from them. It had been five years.

How in the world did Isaiah know cashews were the problem? How did he even come up with the word *cashews*? It's not a word we use often. We don't keep them in the house. By the time he told me what the problem was, it had been only about five minutes since he ate the bar. He took the Benadryl early enough to prevent a severe reaction. I asked him how he knew that cashews were the problem.

"I don't know," he said nonchalantly.

What? "Did a little voice inside your head say 'cashews'?"

"Yes."

"Was it God?"

"Yes."

If you've been keeping up, you know this was not the first time Isaiah heard God communicate with him. He also had a moment at the rehab hospital when God told him not to take his medication anymore. There have been other times when I've asked Isaiah if God told him something, and he looked at me like I was crazy and said no. So I believe him when he says yes. I let him get back to what he was doing and just sat and marveled at our God.

I am still blown away by what happened. What does God have planned for this kid? Eating cashews is a life-threatening deal for Isaiah. God wasn't having it. He wasn't done. Not that day.

I can't help but think about how God knows and cares for each one of us. He has plans for us. Luke 12:7 says, "Indeed, the very hairs of your head are all numbered. Don't be afraid; you are worth more than many sparrows."

Jeremiah 1:5 (ESV) comes to mind too, for this journey Isaiah was on. Before I formed you in the womb I knew you, and before you were born I consecrated you; I appointed you a prophet to the nations."

Okay, Lord, I hear you. I see you. I'm watching.

We made it through the rest of Friday with no other major events. Hallelujah. We enjoyed a handful of visitors and watched a movie. Overall, it was a good day. Better than the day before.

When I put Isaiah to bed that night, he said, "Mom, work."

"I know, tomorrow we will work and do your therapy. I have to sleep tonight so we can."

"Yes. Go to bed. You need sleep." He was counting the hours before morning.

We prayed, I kissed him goodnight, then went to bed.

As I lay there, I drifted back to that moment of afternoon panic. If Isaiah had not been able to say the word *cashews*, he might have died. Just the second day home from hospitalization for a life-altering event, Isaiah could have had another one. God saved us from another crisis. We were home but not on our own. Amen and amen.

A fleeting thought crossed my mind as my eyelids fell shut—*I'm not the one in charge*. It was going to take some time to get used to that.

CHAPTER 21

GOALS AND MOTHERHOOD

Isaiah slept well overnight, which meant I did too. Because he had been having such trouble sleeping, the doctor had prescribed him sleeping meds. That made a world of difference. Apparently, after a brain injury, sleep is often difficult. Isaiah begged for the meds as an inability to sleep is pretty much torture.

I brought him breakfast, then prepared the shower for him. I thought the whole thing would be more of a challenge than it was. RCP had prepared us well. He showered and dressed with no problems. He was ready to start the day. He looked at me and said, "Work."

I took the printouts that each therapist gave us, and we began. I'm not really a therapist; I just play one when I'm at home.

I wasn't surprised, but it still amazed me how he progressed each day. He had improved some since his last day of therapy at RCP earlier in the week. No setbacks. Initially, the medical staff told us he would take some steps forward and some steps back. We had yet to see a day that hadn't been better than the previous one. Even though he showed moments of disappointment, he always seemed to combat it with something positive. He worked so hard.

Isaiah moved around the house well in his wheelchair, regardless of the small spaces. He insisted that he do most things on his own. That independence was often difficult for me to allow. I was afraid he would get hurt, and I wasn't used to him not wanting or needing me to do every little thing for him. But he was determined. The day we came home, he told us that he would be where he wanted to be in five weeks. He had given himself a goal, and he intended to stick to it. Each day he made sure I stayed on task to do his therapy with him.

I sometimes found myself watching him and the miracle he was. He made my job almost easy. I'm not sure I would have been as strong as I was if he hadn't been as strong as he was. I even marveled at the relationship between our three kids. Most days Olivia was quick to help him with anything he needed. She did whatever he asked her to do without complaint. She would not have done that before. In return, Isaiah showed more concern for her well-being than he did before. It was a little late when he looked at the clock and said, "Olivia, go to bed." I asked him why he told her that, and he said, "It's late. She needs sleep." I had always prayed that our children's love for each other would grow over the years, and I knew that prayer had been answered through a near tragedy. I also knew that at some point, the girls would grow tired of his concern and it could potentially turn ugly.

I know God has big plans for each one of our children. I became more mindful of taking time to appreciate who they are. We all get frustrated with our kids at times, and at times we get more than frustrated. We often take their lives and their presence for granted. I know I did. That night of September 8, I remember feeling so guilty for pushing Isaiah away at times when he wanted a hug. It's not that I didn't love him or want his affection. But he wanted a hug almost every time he walked past me, and he is a big kid. I know I'm irresistible and all, but sometimes I just wanted my space. (I know there are other moms out there who know what I'm talking about.) Now I have a different perspective. I find it easier to choose my battles. I find it easier to delight in the small things they do. Somehow my children are now even funnier to me than they used to be. I decided to look at every hug from one of my children as if it might be the last hug I ever get from them, because it could be the last. "Children are a gift from the Lord; they are a reward from him" (Psalm 127:3 NLT). It was about time we started acting like it.

Three days in, I felt the sleep deprivation of a mother with a newborn. Isaiah slept better than ever Saturday night, but I went to bed too late. Sunday morning I woke with flaming plantar fasciitis. I realized how bad the pain was when I had to jump out of bed to help Isaiah first thing. Not a good way to start the day. I was frustrated that God would allow this to happen to me amid everything else. But I reminded myself that the gratitude I felt having Isaiah alive and well at home with us was more than worth the pain in my foot.

Ozzy and the girls had to be at church early that day, so they left. Isaiah was patient with me and let me go back to bed with ice on my foot for a while. It had been seven Sundays since he and I had been to our Holland Park Church to worship. Isaiah was not quite ready for the crowd. Even though we told him he didn't have to speak, he still felt pressure to do so. We'd take him when he was ready. The good thing was that we could talk to Jesus wherever we were.

The girls had their Ballroom Dance Showcase that same day, and Isaiah didn't want to go, but we explained that he would have no pressure to speak since he didn't know anyone there. He agreed he would go and support his sisters. I think he enjoyed the show more than he would admit, although he did not enjoy the dress Abrianna had on. She looked too much like a woman for his taste. He wasn't alone. Ozzy didn't quite approve either. Dads and brothers—*ugh*!

The rest of the day was nice and calm, and we could relax as a family. I was feeling extra grateful for Ozzy that day. Since we had been home, he had stepped up to do everything I needed or asked of him. I could see he didn't want to create any extra stress for me on top of taking care of Isaiah. I was trying to get better at expressing my appreciation for the wonderful partner he is. God knew what he was doing when he put us together. I am grateful for such a good man.

On that same day, I learned of another young man, Baylor Bramble, who was fighting for his life in Murfreesboro, Tennessee. He had sustained a head injury during a football game. He was sixteen years old, played football, and had a brain bleed. The story had my attention. I couldn't stop thinking about his mother. I knew she wasn't sleeping. I knew she wasn't eating. Tears fell down my face as I felt her pain. I think for the first time, as I empathized with a woman I'd never met, I felt a small portion of what Mary must have felt knowing her son was going to die—not only knowing but watching as He died. The song "Mary, Did You Know?" played on repeat in my head.

Do any of us mothers have any idea what God will call us to endure as the mother of any child? Can we fathom what some of us will have to watch our boys or girls go through? The first chapter of 1 Samuel tells of a woman named Hannah who prayed for a child but promised that she would give him to the Lord. Once he was weaned, she took him to the temple to live, learn, and serve. She literally gave him to the Lord. Are we willing to do the same? That's a tough one. Obviously, we're not going to take our sons to a temple and leave them there the way Hannah did, but we may be asked to allow our children to do God's work in ways we can't imagine. I could never imagine God would have my son serve Him this way.

Every time I laid my eyes on Isaiah, I quietly rejoiced that I didn't have to watch his life be sacrificed. But as I've said before, I knew going into motherhood that he was only on loan, so I am grateful for each day. At the moment I was meditating on these truths, I heard Isaiah downstairs as he watched a football game with his dad. *He gets to watch football. Thank you, Lord.*

I wish the world were full of butterflies, rainbows, and unicorns. I wish that young football players would stop dying from head injuries. I didn't know if it had been happening for decades or if I was just then noticing because a brain bleed at football practice almost took my son. Maybe it's like how right after you get a new car, you notice so many of the cars on the road are the same as yours. They suddenly multiply when they never seemed to be there before. I didn't think that so many football players dying or suffering brain aneurysms at that time was a coincidence. Maybe I was supposed to start paying attention. Possibly Isaiah and (prayerfully) Baylor would be spokesmen for football safety one day when they recovered completely.

We didn't know for sure that Isaiah's brain bleed had stemmed from a football injury, but the sport still had too many deaths and injuries that needed to be addressed. The numbers broke my heart.

So many times, we hear people say, _____ *happened for a reason*. I don't subscribe to the belief that tragedies happen *for* a specific reason—otherwise understood as *God makes them happen*. No. God does, however, *allow* suffering. Like I've said before, God doesn't want to see us hurt. He hurts when we hurt.

Nevertheless, He sees a bigger picture we can't possibly fathom, and He allows situations to work for a greater good and for His glory. When we are the ones tragedy happens to, it seems unfair. Maybe the mother of another boy in Texas I read about—a boy who died from a brain aneurysm—would think it was easy for me to say tragedies work to God's glory because my son is still alive. I get it. Maybe I can look at the mother of the kid who sustained only a concussion and say, *That's too easy. You have no idea.* But I'm not going to because I "know that in all things God works for the good of those who love him, who have been called according to his purpose" (Romans 8:28). I do love Him, and I know we have been called.

That morning, I talked to someone at the RCP outpatient rehabilitation center where Isaiah was supposed to begin his outpatient therapy. They told me there were no openings in the schedule. It could be two to three weeks before they would have room for him to begin. I was frustrated, bordering on angry. They reminded me we were sent home with handouts of exercises to do at home. I said that yes, I remembered, and we were using them, but *I am not a therapist.* I was concerned his progress would slow down because I could not help him correctly. They couldn't help me, so I tried to remember I wasn't the one calling the shots. I prayed we would get in by the following week, then turned my focus to something else.

The week before we left the hospital, Isaiah had been invited to the football D Team cookout, and it was coming up that night. We asked him if he wanted to go, and he answered, "I guess."

We told him that "I guess" was not a good enough answer. We needed a yes or no.

He thought about it. "Yes."

He missed his boys. Like most boys his age, he wanted to be part of something—and he was. He was a part of a wonderful, supportive, loving football family who honored him every chance they had. That night, as we prepared to leave, Isaiah informed me that I wasn't allowed to go. He wanted it to be just him and his dad.

Umm. "Excuse me?"

"You stay. I don't want you. Dad go."

"Okay, well, that's not happening. I'm going."

This kid insisted I stay home. He believed it would only be the guys. Ha! I told him I didn't care what he thought, that I gave birth to him, and I'd been taking care of him, doing everything for him, and I was going whether he liked it or not. He had some nerve. The funny thing is, his insistence didn't even hurt my feelings. I mean, the kid had a brain injury. He wasn't in his right mind. He continued trying to convince me to stay home, and I continued to walk out the door.

When we were close to the school, my friend and team mom, Siobhan, texted me to ask how Isaiah was doing. I let her know we were almost there and to please make sure the boys didn't crowd Isaiah once we arrived. I didn't want the experience to overwhelm him. She was also thoughtful enough to ask if they should turn the loud music down. When Isaiah rolled in, the room grew quiet. Each of his teammates lined up, and one by one, they approached him, giving him pounds, handshakes, hugs, and high fives.

Isaiah had a profoundly serious look on his face most of the time. I think he was emotional. One of the boys did manage to make him laugh at one point. I caught a few of the other mothers' watery eyes and warned them not to go there. I was not ready for the ugly cry to make an appearance. I had been a substitute teacher to some of these boys—and expected to be again. I couldn't let them see how soft I was. One boy in particular, who always gave me a hard time in class when I was subbing, gave me the biggest, longest hug and told me I needed to come back and sub for him. I think he was trying to break me. It might have worked.

Isaiah enjoyed his time with friends. Toward the end of the party, the coach presented him with a beautiful football signed by the whole team. Though Isaiah never made it to even one game, they gave him the honor of being the team captain. He led well.

On our way home, I asked him if he felt like a celebrity with all the cameras and cell phones pointed at him the whole time.

He looked shocked. "What? Oh man, I was eating!"

We assured him that no one took a picture of him eating, and he settled down. Now he knows what celebrities deal with.

We are happy he enjoyed the event and were beyond thankful for the love and support Isaiah's teammates, coaches, and the community of Mauldin continued to show him. Through this struggle, Isaiah had seen so much love. He had seen so much joy. He had seen so much goodness.

Joanna Weaver said it perfectly:

> If Jesus Christ can turn death into life, sorrow into gladness, suffering into triumph—then nothing truly bad can ever touch our lives again. Not really. Unfortunate things may happen. Difficulties may come. But it all becomes fodder for a greater work, a more glorious glory.[2]

Those would be good words to remember as Isaiah peered over the precipice at his shattered dreams.

---

2   Joanna Weaver, *At the Feet of Jesus: Daily Devotions to Nurture a Mary Heart* (WaterBrook, 2012).

CHAPTER 22

SHATTERED DREAMS

The cold, wet, dreary Tuesday seemed to wrap a heavy blanket over both Isaiah and me. I was thankful the weather affected him the same way it affected me because I needed more sleep. The downside was that it was hard to get up and do what had to be done for the day. The good side was that once we were up, we were motivated, knowing we had wasted a lot of time.

My mom came over to work with Isaiah. She was the perfect person to handle his speech therapy while we were home. The time she spent with Isaiah was a blessing. At one point during a break, Isaiah looked at her seriously and said, "Nani, you too fast. Make me sick." It took us a minute to figure out what he was talking about, but finally, we understood he was telling her that she had driven too fast the day before when she took him to her house. He was upset about it. She denied the allegation of course, and they went back and forth debating her driving skills. Finally, we explained that the next time he had an issue with someone's driving, he needed to say it right then and there, not stew over it and bring it up later. He agreed he would do that the next time. He laughed, then apologized.

It seems like the dampness of rain also tends to dampen every part of the day. Not necessarily in a bad way, but difficult circumstances often seem a little heavier and calmer on rainy days. Sometimes the rain mutes the sounds of restlessness. It's as though you don't even know how to exist on days like that, so you just sit and think.

That day, I felt as if I were holding my breath. I was holding it, waiting to see what God had to say. The tension in my shoulder muscles were contracting in a painful way. Where were we, and where did He have us going? I allowed God to guide us in the direction we needed to go as we made decisions for outpatient therapy. Two to three weeks was too long to wait. I believed I could cause damage to Isaiah if I didn't show him the proper way to do his therapy exercises. Thankfully, we had wise friends who gave us second and third opinions, helping us make the decision to branch out from the one facility we were so attached to.

Throughout this journey, I have had many new experiences. There have been some disappointments. There have been many surprises. I discovered inside strangers the most loving hearts I had ever seen. I also encountered people whose motives weren't entirely clear, who responded less than amicably. I had learned of a child named Baylor, who was not my own, whose life seemed to have been thrown into the mix of my heart's desires. I became afraid I would be disappointed with God's answer concerning his life, but I found a quote from Hannah Whitall Smith that helped me put some of these things into perspective as I continued to enter unchartered territory:

> We must meet our disappointments, our persecutions, our malicious enemies, our provoking friends, our trials and temptations of every sort, with an attitude of surrender and trust. We must spread our wings and "mount up" to the "heavenly places in Christ" above them all, where they will lose their power to harm or distress us.[3]

I did my best to trust God above it all.

My control issues kept rearing up, too, as I kept trying to figure out what God was doing and guess His reasons for doing so. I dug deep into these verses from the book of Isaiah:

---

3   Hannah Whitall Smith, *The Christian's Secret of a Happy Life: Life-Changing Perspectives on Faith* (Barbour Books, 2019).

For my thoughts are not your thoughts, neither are your ways my ways," declares the Lord. "As the heavens are higher than the earth, so are my ways higher than your ways and my thoughts than your thoughts. (Isaiah 55:8–9)

Some people may be offended by that verse, as we tend to think more of ourselves than we should, but I find it comforting. I don't have to have the answers, but I can trust an omniscient God to handle the details for me. I have to let them go. Hand them over—and don't take them back.

On Wednesday we worked on getting our groove back. Our physical therapist friend, Chuck, set up a PT appointment for us at a local facility, getting us in that very morning. So we went out into the misty drizzle. I was extremely thankful it wasn't full-on raining like the day before. Getting in and out of the car and packing up a wheelchair would not have been easy in the pouring rain. We did fine, and the drizzling rain felt good. You know something had changed in this Black girl's life if I let water drizzle on my head!

Soon after we came home, a good friend brought Isaiah and me lunch. We visited with her until my mom came over to do speech therapy with Isaiah. While she did that, I resumed some regular mom activities and picked Olivia up from school. We even had a chance to visit one of our favorite places, Hobby Lobby, where we found the pieces and parts for her Halloween costume.

Later that night as I was putting Isaiah to bed, he tried to explain something to me. He said the word *medication*, something about sleep, and rattled off a few numbers. He was having a tough time putting his thoughts and words together. He became frustrated that I couldn't understand what he wanted to tell me. I told him I could see he was tired and needed to get more sleep so his brain would work better and give him the words he wanted to say. He had been skipping naps, which were vital to his recovery. I told him we would revisit what he was trying to tell me in the morning.

His whole face drooped, and his eyes watered.

It broke me, so I backtracked. "I'm so sorry I couldn't understand what you were trying to tell me, Isaiah. Let's try again."

Finally, I figured out he was concerned that Ozzy had given him only half a tablet of his sleeping medication. He feared it would affect his sleep. I reassured him it would be okay and that he had slept well with only half the night before. He seemed satisfied, and I felt relieved. He still looked sad, so I asked, "Does it upset you that you have such a hard time talking?"

"Yes," he answered sadly.

"I understand. That has to be really frustrating."

The crease between his eyebrows deepened. "Mom, I don't want this."

His words shot an arrow straight through my heart. "I know, Isaiah. I'm sorry. I don't want this for you either, but I'm proud of you. You are doing so well, and you're getting better every day. Can you tell you're doing better each day?"

He smiled. "Yes."

"I'm glad, because you're amazing and strong." I hugged him and told him it was okay to cry if he needed to and to always tell me if he felt frustrated. He agreed he would. He didn't cry, but he did give me that sweet smile of his, where his eyes soften with understanding, love, and even a sparkle. *Ugh*. He melts my heart. I think he just wanted to know it was okay to have the feelings he had.

I prayed Isaiah would do the things he's always wanted and planned to do (other than football), but I was fully aware he might have some shattered dreams. I saw one dream shattered even then. I knew it would get pieced back together one day, but that's not the case for everyone. I had read a quote earlier that day from Joanna Weaver about shattered dreams. I think most of us have at least one.

> Jesus steps down into our pain and gathers us in His arms. He doesn't chastise us for what we've gone through or insist we explain the death [shattered dream] we now mourn. He holds us close and weeps over what sin and death have done to us, His beloved. He doesn't look down on our wild-eyed nakedness,

because Jesus understands. He has walked where we've walked, and He has felt what we've felt.

"For we do not have a high priest who is unable to sympathize with our weakness," Hebrews 4:15 ESV tells us. We have a tender Savior with a heart big enough to handle our sorrow and gentle hands able to carry our pain.[4]

I was thankful I had help to carry the pain I felt for Isaiah. What an enormous burden it would have been if I couldn't hand it over to Jesus. Because of Him, I could still find joy. I knew the experience would make an amazing man out of an already amazing boy. I looked forward to seeing his growth and delighted in the changes I could see in him taking place right before my eyes. What a glorious sight.

—⁓—

Though I worked hard to hold on to optimism, getting up in the morning became harder and harder. The reality of my therapy diligence shattered my ideal vision of what I thought it would be before we left the hospital. I was losing steam but couldn't let Isaiah know. We seemed to be getting up later and later each day. We needed someplace to go. He appeared to feel the same. He wasn't waking up as he did the previous week, asking to work. This particular day when I had given him exercises to do in the morning, he groaned. After a few sets of exercises on the couch, he slumped over and lay on his side.

"Isaiah, are you actually tired or feeling lazy?"

"Lazy," he said.

"Yeah, me too."

With his face buried in the cushion of the couch, he said, "Get up, Isaiah, get up, Isaiah, get up, Isaiah." Then he answered himself. "But I can't."

I told him I found it a bit frightening he was answering himself. We both laughed and laughed.

---

4   Joanna Weaver, *Lazarus Awakening: Finding Your Place in the Heart of God* (WaterBrook Press, 2011).

Then he sat up and said, "Mom. Hospital."

"You want to go back to the hospital?"

"Yes."

I knew exactly what he meant. He missed having a strict schedule to follow every day. I missed it too. It was hard to get motivated being in the comfort of our own home. Then I realized I hadn't told him about the call that morning from RCP. They were able to get him in sooner than they thought. I told him he would start again with them the following week.

"Yes! Reagan, Shawn, Carey?" he asked.

His shoulders dropped when I told him that the therapists he had grown to know and love would not be the therapists he would have at the new location, but I was sure they'd be great, and he'd like them once they became acquainted. I was looking forward to getting into a better routine and having the pressure of therapy coming off me. Some days I failed. I didn't push him as I thought I would. I was so tired, and I wanted it to be someone else's job. We had done a decent amount of therapy, but we could have done more. The "total failure" label crept into view. How long would this process be my required total focus?

Later in the afternoon, I took him with me to pick Olivia up from school, then ran a few errands. He was miserable most of the time in the car. The car ride turned his stomach, and he complained about it the whole way. Once we pulled in the driveway, he said, "Never go in car again." His sensitivity must have been a side effect of the brain injury. He felt terrible, and I prayed it wouldn't last forever. I was sure he'd change his mind about the car the next day.

He was able to focus on something other than complaining when his friend Nicholas came over. Together they played Isaiah's favorites— Sorry and Connect Four. Both boys hated to lose, so they played over and over again.

Then I had a moment when talking to my mom about preparing Isaiah for homebound learning. She told me she had spoken with his school counselor, and they discussed that when he went back to school, he would probably have an Individualized Educational Plan (IEP) with a list of accommodations and possibly school district therapists to come work with him at school. She was certified and approved to be his homebound teacher, so he would get a lot more help and attention than the regular one hour per day he would typically get in that program. His way of learning would be totally different. It was another dose of reality about how much life had changed for Isaiah.

Isaiah had been an honor student who would often check out a three-hundred-page book from the school library, then have it entirely read by the time he went to bed that same night. This was a boy who earned the first chair position in the school band playing the trumpet. This was a boy who could transform himself into any character in a lead role in the school play. Now, he struggled to read an elementary-level book, couldn't use his fingers to play his trumpet, and couldn't memorize the lines of a script, much less speak them to an audience. Talk about shattered dreams. *God, please put the pieces back together.*

While I wholeheartedly believed God would put the pieces back together, I also knew He might not put them together the same way they were before. I knew He had the power to change the shape of some of those pieces. He could also switch them around or remove some and still have a whole person. I had to accept the changed person Isaiah had become and encourage him as he learned to accept the changed person he was.

At the time, I didn't think I needed to mourn what had been lost because what he could gain was so brilliant. I remembered how a few weeks before that day, all I wanted was to see Isaiah smile again. I received that gift and continued to see many more every single day. I couldn't know what the future held, but I could rest in God's peace and love. Singer and songwriter Laura Story wrote this in her devotional book *What if Your Blessings Come through Raindrops?*:

> Some things in life are uncertain: health may vanish; wealth may disappear; success may be fleeting, and the victories we hold most dear may, in time, be transformed into bitter defeats. But in a

world of uncertainties, one thing is certain. God loves us. And that one fact can make all the difference.[5]

I understood what she was saying. I knew the truth: For the Lord is good and his love endures forever; his faithfulness continues through all generations. (Psalm 100:5) I would hold tight to that Scripture when I felt like my pieces were scattered.

---

5   Laura Story, *What if Your Blessings Come through Raindrops?* (Worthy, 2012).

CHAPTER 23

WHO'S IN CHARGE?

It was the last session of Isaiah's interim therapy sessions. He had gained more control of his right arm during this interim work, so I thought the decision to get outside help had been justified. I worried about the car ride home, but he didn't seem to get sick this time. Maybe he just needed to readjust to riding in a car.

After we had been home a few minutes, I called a friend. In the middle of our conversation, Isaiah grabbed the phone from me, put it to his ear and said, "My mom gotta go."

Wow. That boy actually believed he was in charge. I took the phone back, apologized for his rudeness, hung up, then gave him the side-eye. "You're not the boss of me."

His eyelids drooped in worry. "Mom, you need sleep. Go to sleep."

I did lie down on the couch and take a short nap. *I'm only lying down because I'm tired and want to, not because you're the boss of me.*

He watched me the whole time, making sure I stayed down.

The rest of the day was good. Isaiah read to me and worked with word flashcards. He kept mentioning wanting to be ready for the outpatient rehab program the following week. He understood how much he would improve with regular sessions as he had in the hospital. I think working increased his determination to get back to the activities he loved. I'm sure he was tired of staying home looking at my mug all day. Looking ahead gave Isaiah a glimpse of hope.

Hope was so important to hold on to. Hope gets us through the tough days, no matter if we struggle with something big or small.

I've always felt I could make it through anything if I had an ounce of hope. Max Lucado wrote, "Teach us to set our hopes on heaven, to hold firmly to the promise of eternal life, so that we can withstand the struggles and storms of this world."[6] I was so thankful Isaiah had that kind of hope.

The next day was Halloween, and I woke up with energy, pumped to get to an evening of trick-or-treating and pretending that our family life was the same as it always had been. After breakfast, I worked on the kids' costumes. I always loved making and putting together their costumes, but why, oh why did I always wait until the last minute to start? My best ideas tend to come under pressure.

Isaiah spent the day watching me work and getting fitted for his DJ box. I decided that a DJ costume would work perfectly with his wheelchair. I would build a DJ booth around him, and he could still sit and get around the neighborhood in his wheelchair. But right before I finished most of his costume, Isaiah said, "I don't want to go."

"Excuse me? Are you trying to tell me, after I've been busting my behind all day to finish your costume, that you don't want to go trick-or-treating?"

"Yes, but I'll go."

"Well, do you just want to pass out candy?"

He looked relieved. "Yes."

A few minutes later, he asked me what he was supposed to say.

"You should say happy Halloween."

He practiced saying it a few times. Then he asked, "What else?"

"Well, if you go trick-or-treating, you say, trick or treat."

He practiced that for several minutes. *Okay then. It's just nerves.*

Ozzy helped with some final touches on Isaiah's costume, and I finished up Olivia's. I was so thankful Abrianna had her own ideas for a costume and worked on that herself. Though we were late, we finished the costumes and headed to my parents' house for trick-or-treating in

---

6   Max Lucado quote found in Laura Story's *What if Your Blessings Come Through Raindrops?* (Worthy, 2012).

their neighborhood as we did every year. After eating dinner, Isaiah decided to join the adventure with his sisters, cousins, and friends. They were all impressed with his costume. The black DJ booth fit perfectly over his wheelchair. He might have had the best costume out there.

Not too long into trick-or-treating, though, Isaiah decided he wanted to go back to his Nani and Papa's house. So we headed back. He didn't seem upset to miss hanging out more with the other kids. I asked him later why he didn't want to keep trick-or-treating. He said it wasn't as much fun in a wheelchair. His words pierced my heart, but he seemed to be okay with it. I said, "Well, you look really good." He smiled and agreed.

The next day Isaiah and I planned to go back to church for the first time since his brain bleed. Although his eyes lit up when we talked about going and worshiping with all his friends and "framily," I could see a crease of worry in his forehead. I wish I could have taken away his anxiety over speaking.

I reminded him of God's response to Moses's fear of speaking, found in Exodus 4. God will always equip us with what we need to do His will or to simply get along and survive each day. Whenever I am insecure about any of my abilities, I try to remember Moses. Whenever Isaiah gets insecure about *his* abilities, I will remind him of Moses and that God is the same God today as He was then and will always be. Isaiah, you're not in charge. God will help you speak.

The next morning my eyes popped open. I lay in bed and stared at the ceiling. I had a hard time waking up, but I'd been looking forward to Sunday all week. Isaiah was ready to go back to church. I mostly looked forward to watching him worship. I jumped up and fussed at everyone else to get going, but we were still late. I walked with Isaiah into the youth class and had planned to stay, but I realized he was okay and I could leave him there as I would have before September 8. So I did, then went to the adult class meeting in another part of the building.

Afterward, I was late getting to the main service, but when I walked in and went to sit with the rest of my family, I saw Isaiah a few rows ahead of me, not sitting in his wheelchair, but *standing* along with the youth and the rest of the congregation while we sang. I almost lost it. He was standing. It wasn't a shock to see him standing, as I see him stand up every day. It hit me differently that he was standing along with his friends like that—in church. God is good.

Further into the service, our pastor, Matt Atnip, went up on stage to give his lesson. He had on a hoodie and mentioned he was a bit hot. So he took it off, revealing his #coollikeisaiah T-shirt underneath. That was touching enough, but when he knelt on his knees and thanked God for Isaiah's life, I cried. I cried because I felt deep gratitude toward God for saving Isaiah's life. I cried because Matt's tender heart and prayer touched mine. We made it through worship, although not without a few more tears. It was wonderful to be back with our church family.

At bedtime, I asked Isaiah what his favorite part of going back to church was.

He smiled. "All of it, and cane."

I was confused. "Do you want a cane?"

That wasn't it. He kept saying cane then man. I wasn't getting it. Finally, he said, "Man cane."

Oh! He was talking about a man with a cane. I thought about it some more, then realized he was talking about Scott Ragin, who had visited him in the hospital. He was at church that day, and Isaiah was happy to see him. It gave him comfort to know others had dealt with the same things he was dealing with. I imagine that camaraderie would be comforting for any of us. So seeing Scott was one of the best parts of his Sunday.

Hopefully, the next day would be just as good. It would be the first day of therapy with the new RCP outpatient therapists he would stay with until he didn't need them anymore—until he was more in charge of his own body. I looked forward to meeting the people who would become a part of our extended family like the therapists before them. Isaiah was ready.

I went to sleep that night giving praise and thanksgiving for all the Lord had done.

> Shout with joy to the Lord, all the earth!
> Worship the Lord with gladness.
> Come before him, singing with joy.
> Acknowledge that the Lord is God!
> He made us, and we are his.
> We are his people, the sheep of his pasture.
> Enter his gates with thanksgiving;
> go into his courts with praise.
> Give thanks to him and praise his name.
> For the Lord is good.
> His unfailing love continues forever,
> and his faithfulness continues to each generation. (Psalm 100 NLT)

CHAPTER 24

FEELS LIKE RAIN

We woke up early and made it to the first day of official outpatient rehab. We had to be there by 8:30 a.m. My disposition reflected the pouring rain. It's not easy to deal with a kid in a wheelchair in the rain. I had one of those *Really, God?* moments, but I put on my big-girl pants and handled it.

I was exhausted. I had been stretched beyond belief for two months. Before our journey began, I would have thought being so tired would make me miserable all around. On that day, though, even as parenthood stretched me beyond what I knew I could endure, I had joy. This joy must have been how Abraham felt when God told him he didn't have to sacrifice his son Isaac. I bet parenting seemed a lot easier to him after that. Though such hardship and sacrifice can be difficult to bear, I have found it to be a gift. When we step inside the experience of potential loss, the reality of recovery becomes a gift. I was thankful for such an incredible gift.

Monday night—the night before—when I hugged Olivia, she told me I was getting sick. I felt fine, so I didn't pay much attention. She often says odd things. But the following morning, even after a good night's sleep, I could hardly keep my eyes open. I asked Isaiah if it was okay with him for me to take a nap, and if he needed me, he could call. He who is the commander of my sleep permitted me to do so. I woke up several times to check on him, but I didn't totally get up until 12:30 p.m. It took me a while to realize I actually didn't feel good. Later that evening, I asked Olivia why she had thought I was getting sick.

She looked at me as if I should have known. "Because you had that aroma."

The force is strong with that one.

But at the time, without her skills to detect my own illness, I finally pulled myself out of bed and put some clothes on. I looked out the window. The gray November sky had subdued the sun, but that day, the clouds seemed more like a low ceiling than a menacing storm. I told Isaiah we were going out. I apologized for being asleep for so long. He was very understanding. We had to go to the Department of Motor Vehicles to get him a handicapped parking tag, so he had his first experience waiting in that notorious line. He was required to get a state ID first, so he also had the experience of signing his name on the little electronic box. It took about five tries. He couldn't write small enough to get both his first and last name in, so the woman behind the counter told him he could just write his first initial and last name. She didn't know that two months before, he didn't even know *how* to write his name. He was frustrated, but I was proud of him for doing it.

After he positioned his wheelchair in front of the camera, he stood up to get his picture taken, but with the wheelchair behind him, he was too close to the camera. The woman asked him to sit down, and she would adjust the camera. He was disappointed. He wanted to do it the way everyone else does. A sharp pang gripped my heart. He so badly wanted to be normal, and the experience lit a fire under him. On our way home, he told me he wanted to be walking by December 25. It seemed a reasonable goal. God had helped him get to where he was, and God could take him further.

I also had to drag Isaiah to Abrianna's orthodontist appointment, and when she was finished, we were in a rush to get to the next place we had to go. As soon as we got to the car, Isaiah informed me he had to go to the bathroom. *Seriously?* It might not have been raining at that moment, but everything *felt* like rain. My *wrath* was about to rain down on his behind. I informed him we were going back into the orthodontist's office because it was easier to go there than someplace else. He told me he would hold it. Oh no. Not a good idea.

"Isaiah, we're going back in now."

He had the nerve to argue with me. "No. I will wait." He leaned forward from his chair and opened the car door to get inside before I made it over to him. The door bumped the car next to us. It didn't do any damage, but I swung my head around and glared at him with flaming eyes.

I closed the door, moved in behind him, and pushed him back toward the building. Once we were inside the first set of doors, he had the audacity to put his foot down so we couldn't go any further. He refused to go. We had moved past the newborn stage straight to the terrible twos.

I had to get down to his level—in his face. I then gave him five seconds to get it together. I'm not sure what I would have done if he didn't lift his foot, but I had five seconds to figure it out. To top it off, I thought I felt a drop of rain. I finally maneuvered him through the door and practically threw him and that wheelchair through the bathroom doors. I didn't have patience for his attitude, and he was making me late.

We avoided the actual rain, if not the metaphorical kind, survived the day, and made it to bedtime. When I was saying goodnight, Isaiah said out of the blue, "I have joy." That boy could find joy even in the rain. It was like God spoke through him sometimes to let me know I was doing okay and that He was covering Isaiah.

My eyes filled with tears. My anger had evaporated. "I'm so glad, Isaiah. I know it's been hard. You're amazing."

Elisabeth Elliot said, "God gives to us a heavenly gift called joy, radically different in quality from any natural joy."[7] I could see that in Isaiah. When he was frustrated or mad at me, and his circumstances weren't what he thought they would be, he still found the kind of joy Jesus spoke about: "These things I have spoken to you, that my joy may be in you, and that your joy may be full" (John 15:11 ESV). I am

---

7   Elisabeth Elliot quote as found in Laura Story's *What if Your Blessings Come through Raindrops?* (Worthy, 2012).

thankful Isaiah was able to find that joy. Yet I couldn't help but wonder if that would last. He had been dealt some tough stuff. All we could do was take one step at a time and expect the best.

The next morning I awoke to the same gloominess as the day before. Where was the sun? It would have been so much easier to get up if the sun had beamed me out of bed. It was day two of outpatient therapy. I went to get Isaiah up and pulled the covers off him, but he wanted to go back to sleep. I reminded him it was therapy day. He insisted on sleeping. So I put the covers back over him and said nonchalantly, "That's okay, Isaiah. You go back to sleep. I guess you don't want to be walking on your own by Christmas. I'll see you later."

He groaned something that sounded like okay and sat up.

There was no reason to argue some days. Since we had plenty of time, I set out his clothes, then left his room. I wanted to see if he could get dressed entirely on his own, and guess what? He did. All by himself. I was thrilled. That was going to make mornings go so much smoother for me.

Leaving the house was more manageable. Even though it was damp, dreary, and threatened rain, it wasn't raining. So getting in and out was less complicated. Each therapist gave Isaiah comprehensive evaluations, testing to see how much he could do. He was incredibly proud of himself during his OT evaluation when his therapist Shannon tested the strength of his nondominant hand, which had become the hand he used the most. His numbers showed above-average strength. He about gave himself another brain bleed, though, as he squeezed the testing contraption as hard as he could.

After therapy, we enjoyed lunch with Ozzy at a pizza place near rehab. It was nice to be out like regular people. Isaiah was tired and lay down in the booth a few times—as a toddler would. I asked him if he wanted to take a nap when he got home, and he gave me an enthusiastic yes. Then he fell asleep in the car on the way home. When we pulled into the driveway, I asked him if he was ready for a nap.

"No! I slept. I'm not tired."

Well, *I* was tired, so I lay down to rest while Isaiah watched football with Ozzy. As for me, I'd had more than enough tackling for the past several days. And I knew there'd be more ahead.

CHAPTER 25

PARTIAL SIGHT

When I woke up the next day, the rainclouds darkening my countenance had lifted, and the birds were singing. It was the day I would take Isaiah to see the man who had saved his life. Although Dr. Troup is one of the most important people to have ever entered his life, Isaiah didn't remember him. So when I told him to get up so we could go see Dr. Troup, he didn't budge. But when I told him Dr. Troup was the man who saved his life, he leaped out of bed (well, almost).

We made it to the doctor's office, and while we were waiting, a sweet woman came up to us and told me she had been praying for Isaiah. Her little girl had broken her neck in an accident on the water, so she could understand what I was going through. Soon after we met her, one of Dr. Troup's staff called out Isaiah's name to take him back for his appointment.

As I followed Isaiah down the hall, tears welled up. The night of September 8 replayed in my mind, and it felt as though I were walking in slow motion. All that fear, heartache, and gratitude swelled up again in me. In my mind, I was back in the room where I had sat with Ozzy, our family, and thirty or so members of our "framily," eyes locked onto Dr. Troup seated in the middle of the room telling us what he would try to do for our son. I remembered how I stopped breathing for a moment when he told us that Isaiah could die. He never minced his words. He presented us with a potential prognosis that was difficult to hear, but he delivered it tenderly. He was humble, and I remembered how that gave me comfort.

Looking back, I realized that just as God had prepared me to lose Isaiah from the day he was born, Dr. Troup had done the same. Being aware from the beginning of what I could lose allowed me to find gratitude for a rescued life that I'm not sure I would have found otherwise. Sometimes God has to allow us to be shaken up a bit to line us back up with His will.

I brought my mind back to the present, refocused on where I was walking, and followed the nurse and Isaiah into a room. We waited there for Dr. Troup. When he walked in, I immediately stood up and hugged him. I didn't cry as I thought I would. I was delighted to see him and full of gratitude. The visit went well. Isaiah's walking progress impressed him. He took his time with us, assessing Isaiah's brain function. It was then we discovered that Isaiah could see only directly in front of him and to the left. Everything past the center and to the right was dark. He had only partial sight. Dr. Troup personally called an ophthalmologist while we were sitting there to ask his opinion about what Isaiah needed. I love him. We finished that appointment with a new item on our healing checklist—something else for my heart to hurt over. But we left feeling thankful.

I also had an appointment at the beauty shop. Isaiah sat there with me for about an hour while my stylist fixed the disaster on top of my head. He didn't complain once. It was training ground for marriage. You're welcome, future wife of my son.

On our way home, we had a tough conversation. Isaiah wanted to know about his brain injury. He tried to understand what it was and how it happened. We talked about how difficult it was for him to focus when too much was going on. I found the injury exceedingly difficult to explain in a way he could understand, and I had tried to explain it before. He became agitated with me when I suggested that football had been part of the problem. He insisted they weren't hitting that day, so an impact couldn't have been what caused it. I explained that I believed the years of hitting had weakened his blood vessels, ultimately leading to bleeding on his brain. He said he understood, then became noticeably quiet. No doctor had confirmed my belief. Nevertheless, it was what I believed to be true.

That night we enjoyed a wonderful dinner that The New York Butcher Shoppe sent us. They had committed to feeding us every Thursday for several weeks. We were blessed by their meals and touched by their generosity.

As I headed toward bed, I again thought back to Dr. Troupe and the night we met him. The peace I had felt was not because I knew Dr. Troup was the man behind the hands operating on Isaiah but because I knew God was behind the man behind the hands operating on Isaiah. Though I remained optimistic about Isaiah's future, I knew he could have some struggles for a long time or the rest of his life. I did my best not to worry because I knew God had been with him every step of the way and would not leave him. As for the future, I decided to rest in this truth spoken by Joni Eareckson Tada:

> The best we can hope for in this life is a knothole peek at the shining realities ahead. Yet, a glimpse is enough. It's enough to convince our hearts that whatever suffering and sorrows currently assail us aren't worthy in comparison to that which waits over the horizon.[8]

I know others are going through similar journeys to ours. For all of us, Psalm 31:24 (NKJV) says, "Be of good courage, And He shall strengthen your heart, All you who hope in the Lord."

—m—

Friday felt different. It was taking a lot for me to get Isaiah out of bed every morning.

He said he was ready to work hard in therapy, but his goals weren't motivating him to jump out of bed as they had been. I kept a keen eye on him, wanting to make sure no depression was creeping in.

---

8 Quoted by Joni Eareckson Tada found in Laura Story's *What if Your Blessings Come Through Raindrops?* (Worthy, 2012).

When I decided in the hospital to keep him off meds, I did it based on what I felt God was telling me at the time. But even when we're confident about God's leading, we still only have partial sight of what lies ahead. It's wise to continue coming back to God to discover if He has inserted any detours on our journey. Isaiah's fantastic attitude made the situation easier for me and gave me a more positive outlook. But God does allow us to struggle with emotions at times. They have a purpose and can remind us of our need for Him.

On our way to therapy, I asked Isaiah a couple of times if he felt okay. His face didn't look right to me—his light seemed dim. He said he was just tired, but I wanted to make sure. So I found some bumpin' music on the radio. I knew if he were okay, he would perk up and start singing and dancing in his seat. He did perk up and reacted the way I anticipated he would, so I relaxed. My professional medical evaluation was solid.

He did well in therapy and seemed to perk up as the morning went on, while I was the one who became a bit weepy. I could see that Isaiah was getting impatient with his progress. Especially with his speech. At least once a day, he would say, "I want to talk." Speaking had become even more important to him than walking. He struggled to get out a complete sentence. There were many thoughts he couldn't communicate effectively. *Never mind* was becoming one of his most common expressions. He'd had a God-given gift of public speaking and had never been afraid to speak in front of anyone. So I knew this battle and loss were hurting him. My main prayer was that his speech would come back faster than it was currently and that he could at least figure out different ways of getting his thoughts across to us until he reclaimed his words.

After therapy, we grabbed lunch, then headed to see the ophthalmologist Dr. Troup's office had set us up with. Dr. Johnson at Jervey Eye Group was fantastic. He asked me to tell him Isaiah's story, and I had to chuckle to myself when he responded to something I said with, "Oh yes, the great Healer." Of course, he knew the Lord. That's how our story goes. I continue to be in awe of the way God orchestrates our days. I can't help but think of Hebrews 12:1, which talks about being "surrounded by such a great cloud of witnesses." When our story is told years from now, all the people I have spoken of will be characterized by that verse.

We learned that Dr. Johnson could do nothing about the parts of Isaiah's vision that were affected. He said we would watch it over time, and the part of his brain that controls the vision might heal just like everything else. I prayed that it would because the vision loss could ultimately affect his safety when driving, among other things.

But in that prayer was another lesson for me. We all have experiences that create a limited vision of our lives or the lives of others. That partial sight creates danger because it affects how we make decisions and sometimes leads to trouble. That's why we've got to pray for God to allow us to see what's true and honoring to Him, so we don't head in the wrong direction.

Isaiah seemed more like himself that afternoon, but I still discerned fear creeping into my spirit. Maybe that's why I felt weepy most of the day. What I know about my fear is that if I trust God with every part of me, there is no need for it. Sometimes I have to say out loud, "God, I trust you, no matter what." It helps to say that out loud. I know God's will is good. I may not understand it, but I choose to embrace its goodness. So I can agree with Max Lucado, who said, "Faith is often the child of fear."[9] May it be so.

I have found that the bigger and scarier something is, the bigger my faith tends to be. For some reason, the bigger something is, the easier it is for me to hand it over to God. It's the smaller things that I mistakenly think I can control, which are when the situation tends to get out of control. I must continually remind myself that if I can trust Him with the big things, I can certainly trust Him with the small ones. How in the world do people live this life without a Savior? He speaks to me in so many ways, but that day He spoke through His

9   Max Lucado quote found in Laura Story's *What if Your Blessings Come Through Raindrops?* (Worthy, 2012).

Word: "For I am the Lord your God who takes hold of your right hand and says to you, Do not fear; I will help you'" (Isaiah 41:13). God is so good. I will continue to trust the Lord to see what I cannot and allow Him to lead me.

CHAPTER 26

PLANS TO SPEAK

Tuesday was one of those mornings. The sun took a long time to make an appearance, so Isaiah and I did too. I needed extra rest, so I had him hang out with me in my room for a while. He worked on Luminosity brain games while I caught a few more z's. I loved hanging out with Isaiah. Before the brain injury, he was always a mild, sweet kid, but he seemed to have become even more so. His heart was so tender. Late morning, we pulled out his therapy binder and found a list of recommended games. Connect Four and Scrabble were on the list, so we played those for a while. Connect Four seems like a simple game, but Isaiah had some kind of crazy strategy where he created multiple ways of winning regardless of where I moved. I think that part of his brain may have been supercharged.

In between games, I had him do some PT. It was hard, but he knew that he had to do it if he wanted to walk well by Christmas—a little over six weeks away. A friend brought dinner over early, and while she was there, we had a conversation about God's plans for Isaiah. At one point, Isaiah said something about going back to playing football.

Ugh. Help me, Lord. Here it comes. I said firmly and gently, "You're not going to play football."

He looked upset. "Why?"

I tried to explain to him that it wasn't going to happen.

His face contorted in all kinds of ways. "What? Why?"

Again, I tried to explain that it wasn't safe. I finally told him that we would talk about it later. *That will be a tough conversation.* He still doesn't completely understand all of it. Ozzy and I have continued telling him that many of his struggles and losses were temporary, but it's hard for him to understand there are things he won't be able (or allowed) to do. We needed to pray about how to approach all of that with him, but now was not the time to have that conversation. I did tell him that I wanted him to be talking to God about his life and what God wanted him to do. I figured maybe he would come to the same conclusions without us.

Shortly after that brief conversation, we had to leave to go to Abrianna's school for a parent basketball meeting. I appreciated that Isaiah didn't complain when I dragged him everywhere I went. I wasn't comfortable leaving him at home alone, and he understood that. He sat patiently through the meeting and admired Abrianna's new basketball shoes when we were in the car. I choked up a moment when I thought about him not playing basketball this season. The thing is, Isaiah was not sad. He was *still* full of joy. He knew that he couldn't do some things at that time, but he looked forward to doing more in the future. That's why I had no plans to steal his joy at that time by continuing to tell him there were things he couldn't do.

He shared with me that he planned to speak at our church on his birthday. His next birthday was on Saturday, May 14, so we planned his speaking debut for Sunday, May 15. A weight lifted from my soul after hearing his plans. It seemed perfect. He knew he had a story to tell and people to encourage and inspire. He continued to encourage and inspire me every single day. As often as I could, I reminded Isaiah that God had a plan for him. He kept telling me he knew that, but I will continue to tell him in case he forgets. Jeremiah 29:11 is one of my favorite verses and a truth I wholeheartedly believe for Isaiah and each of us. It says, "For I know the plans I have for you," declares the Lord, "plans to prosper you and not to harm you, plans to give you hope and a future." (Jeremiah 29:11) I hoped and prayed that when Isaiah understood that he wouldn't be able to play football anymore, he would hold on to this Scripture and understand that whatever God had planned for his future is good and perfect and that Isaiah would find peace if he trusted God.

That night, we didn't worry about anything. We enjoyed family time with all of us in the same room. The kids piled in our bed as they used to when we all fit. It didn't last long, but it was good stuff. I felt complete.

—⁓—

Oh, what a beautiful morning! Oh, what a beautiful day. The next morning's sun brought me such joy. Thank you, Lord. We were long overdue. Since Ozzy had the day off, he took Isaiah to therapy, and I was grateful to spend time with my friend Kendra. I felt renewed afterward. She told me some things I needed to know but didn't necessarily want to hear. Authenticity is hard to come by, but when you find a friend who can tell you how it really is, hold on to them.

After my friend time, I headed toward Isaiah's rehab facility, where I relieved Ozzy, who went to have lunch with Olivia at school. I talked to the speech therapist, Jenna, and she told me that Isaiah had improved his score in a specific category by 18 percent in *one session*. He had made that much of an improvement since Monday! She was impressed.

As had become our ritual, I took Isaiah to get lunch after therapy. We decided that since it was such a beautiful day, we didn't want to go home. So we went to church to hang out with the crew there. Isaiah headed straight for his youth minister's office. Charlie was in, and they discussed the best day for Isaiah to speak in front of the church. They bumped it to May 22, but it was on the calendar, and Isaiah was grinning like a Cheshire cat. He knew—and we believed—that he would be able to walk right up those stairs onto the stage and give an eloquent as well as moving testimony. God had only *just* begun with our boy.

After we left the church building, we headed toward Olivia's elementary school so I could handle some business there. I got out of my SUV and took Isaiah's wheelchair out of the back. I wheeled the chair around to Isaiah's side. When I opened the door, he sat looking at me defiantly.

"No. I not go in," he said.

I explained to him that I didn't know how long I would be in there, so he needed to come with me.

"No. I stay here."

I stood there for a few minutes while I begged him to go with me. I knew he had to go to the bathroom, and it was ridiculous to sit in the car and wait.

His eyes filled with tears. "Fine, but I come back to the car."

"Why don't you want to go in? Do you not want to deal with all the people?"

"No."

I completely understood. People can be overwhelming, especially because we were at the elementary school he had attended, and teachers tended to fawn over their previous students. But I didn't have a choice. I wasn't going to leave him in the car. We headed in, and of course, he received a lot of attention. He handled it okay. He understood that people were just so happy to see him alive and doing well. They couldn't help but be joyful when they laid eyes on him. I mean, I'm joyful when I lay eyes on him, and I get to see him every day.

When we got back in the car, I asked him if the attention was *that* bad.

He grinned. "No."

I think Mrs. Floyd was his favorite. She hugged and kissed him and told him how handsome he was. How could he not love that? He remembered when she and her daughter Mia had come to the PICU to sing for him. It was after that visit when we realized he couldn't handle any more visitors. After they finished singing a beautiful song and asked him how he liked it, he pulled the covers over his head. When I asked him about it today, he said he remembered how beautiful their singing was but didn't remember pulling the covers over his head.

We sat there in the car waiting for Olivia while we listened to Christmas music. Yes, it was only the middle of November, and we were listening to Christmas music. I was opposed to that genre, but my son wanted to listen to it, so I let him. That music brought him joy.

And I thought back to something I had heard on the radio that struck a chord with me. A man was talking about Noah and how his story relates to us today. He said that maybe you think God hasn't done anything dramatic in your life for a while, and you've faithfully been living the Christian life, wondering where He is. He said that all you need to do is continue doing the last thing God told you to do. Just like Noah building that ark. Hold your course and carry on. God will finish what He started.

For a long time, I felt that God was silent in my life. For a long time, I was holding my course—going along with what I thought I was supposed to do, but nothing dramatic was happening. I always knew He was there, but I expected more. I wanted to see God in a *big* way. Frequently, my prayer was for Him to increase my faith and to make me *feel* something. I prayed this prayer for over two years, maybe even three or four. On September 8, God answered my prayers, but it was not the answer I was looking for. It was the answer nonetheless.

I try to remember that God's time is not even close to ours. He takes time to rearrange the universe in order to line things up just right to accomplish what He wants for each of us. I imagine that process could take many years.

There are situations God began preparing me for years ago that won't come to fruition until many years in the future. What's interesting is that sometimes what God begins never ends. Sometimes He starts something, finishes it, and then starts something new. I've decided to hold on for the long ride. I thought forward to when Isaiah would make his speaking debut. I wondered if we would learn then about what God had been working on inside him.

And I am certain that God, who began the good work within you, will continue his work until it is finally finished on the day when Christ Jesus returns. (Philippians 1:6 NLT)

Believe that. I do.

CHAPTER 27

WALKING IN FAITH

When I woke up, I could tell it was a gorgeous fall day, but we had a hard time getting up again. It was more difficult on nontherapy days. I think it's because therapy days were so packed with activity that they completely wore us out. At some point late in the morning, as I was coming out of my room, I heard Isaiah. I looked up, and there he was, fully dressed and walking down the stairs. It was normal for him to walk down the stairs and into his wheelchair with my help each day. But without any help or prompting from me, he chose his clothes and put them on, and for me that was like drinking a coffee cup full of profound joy.

After a late breakfast, we played a game of Monopoly. He needed no help with any of the money transactions. That part of his brain had engaged.

Later that evening, while watching Abrianna play in her first high school basketball scrimmage at her school, one of her teammates fell and hit her head on the gym floor. She was in a lot of pain. My heart started beating hard and fast. I found it challenging to breathe. I felt my body begin to rise from the bleachers so I could run onto the court to make sure she was okay, but I stopped. She wasn't my kid. I wanted to scream at the coach to check her eyes. I now know that pupils are telling when it comes to brain injuries.

Instead, I sat in silence, praying she was okay and holding back tears. My whole body felt as if it were in a vice. She was okay as far as we could tell, but I was worried she would have a brain injury, and

I couldn't help but think of what her mom would have to go through. The fact that it upset me so much caught me off guard. I absolutely overreacted internally. I don't think anyone around me could tell that I was about to leap from my seat to freak out over a child who wasn't mine, but I was. Our situation had affected me in ways I hadn't realized. I am much more aware of things that hurt our children's brains and sensitive to all of them. I'm not sure people understand how serious a concussion can be. It's a brain injury. Baylor had a concussion weeks before he ended up unresponsive in a Tennessee hospital. Concussions can be profoundly serious.

Although I never felt that I actively worried about Isaiah, I did internalize some feelings that tried to push their way out on occasion. During that early recovery time, I often had flashbacks to that night and teared up as I thought about the what-ifs and how things could have turned out differently. I knew I shouldn't have been thinking that way, but the replay kept coming up for some reason. Maybe it was a form of worry, which is also a form of fear.

Paul wrote in 2 Timothy 1:7 (NLT), For God has not given us a spirit of fear and timidity, but of power, love, and self-discipline. (2 Timothy 1:7 nlt) I had no reason to worry over anything, especially things that hadn't even happened. Worry is not something that had ever been an issue for me, so I believed the enemy was trying to use it to weaken my faith. Well, I declared he would not win. Regardless of how I felt, I spoke Psalm 56:3 in faith. When I am afraid, I put my trust in you. (Psalm 56:3)

The next day after therapy, Isaiah was thrilled to bring home a walker. He would have skipped home—if the walker had allowed him. He understood it was the next step toward walking without assistance. It gave him more freedom. The following week he would get fitted for special orthotics that would help him walk even better. He also noticed that his speech had improved. He kept saying over and over in his biggest, manliest voice, "I can speak well."

I stayed up late that night. I knew I should have gone to bed earlier, but sometimes it's nice to be up in a quiet house without the kids underfoot. I need that quiet time to be still and sense God's presence. Sometimes I have a hard time feeling Him. More than likely, it's because I'm not still very often. I get distracted by my circumstances or even so disappointed in them that I don't seek Him. I've had times when I sit and pout. During this trial, God made His presence known to me much more vividly and frequently—or maybe I finally decided to take time to acknowledge His presence. Gloria Gaither said, "God walks with us. He scoops us up in His arms or simply sits with us in silent strength until we cannot avoid the awesome recognition that yes, even now, He is here."

What a difference His presence makes. I was able to exist in a place of peace—because of Him. You will show me the way of life, granting me the joy of your presence and the pleasures of living with you forever. (Psalm 16:11 NLT)

Olivia had an early Saturday morning basketball game, and Isaiah wanted to cheer her and her team on. So we dragged ourselves out of bed and went to the game. It was an entertaining game, to say the least, and Isaiah had a lot to yell about. Afterward, we decided to stay out longer, so we headed to Starbucks with the girls and some friends.

Isaiah was quiet and somber-looking, and I wondered if something was wrong. "Are you okay, Isaiah?"

He looked annoyed. "All girls."

I smiled. One day he'd appreciate that. Because we were downtown, Isaiah had to do more walking than he'd done in two months. Our destination wasn't far, but it was still the most he'd walked in a long time. By the time we arrived home, he was exhausted, so he lay down intending to take a nap. He couldn't fall asleep right away, so he asked if he could do yoga. Yep. Yoga. I found a chair yoga video on YouTube and turned it on for him. He did a great job. Maybe it would be his new thing. Perhaps it should be *my* new thing.

After watching Isaiah walk so much that weekend, I started to think about the importance of walking. It's something most of us take for granted. We get up and walk without giving it a second thought.

I no longer take it for granted because I have pain when I walk a lot of the time. Isaiah no longer takes it for granted because he doesn't have much control over his walking or how well he can do it. We are both very intentional about where we walk. We are also careful about where and how we step. Isn't that how we should walk through life?

I read a great story about a youth pastor who had an accident that resulted in his paralysis from the waist down. A man came to visit him not long after and said, "These things sure have a way of coloring our lives, don't they?"

The youth pastor responded with a smile. "Yeah, they sure do, but I get to choose the color."

I decided to choose my color. We can't help what happens to us, but we can choose our response to what happens.

On Monday we started back to therapy. I could tell Isaiah was getting comfortable with his therapists because he showed them his silly, thirteen-year-old boy side. Mondays are long days for us because his psychology appointment is also on Mondays. Though he didn't talk to the psychologist about it, something had changed in Isaiah's brain to make him critical of what he saw in the mirror as well as in pictures. He'd never had a problem concerning self-esteem before. I prayed that he would once again see himself the way God did. He is such a beautiful soul and should always know his value.

That night after enjoying time out with a friend, I went to Isaiah's room to tuck him in and pray with him. I always loved to talk and snuggle with him at that hour, and sometimes he did as well, but sometimes he was too tired and wanted me to get out so he could go to sleep. Like that night. I missed him being little. I missed all my kids being little, but since Isaiah had become man-sized, I missed "little Isaiah" even more. When he was a little boy, the most he had to worry about was where his Rescue Rangers action figures were and if they had all the pieces to their uniforms. He didn't worry about anything unbecoming he thought he might see in the mirror. I don't even think he looked in the mirror as a little boy. Our views change so dramatically as we grow older. I wish we could be children a bit longer than we are. I thought about what Jesus had to say about children:

> At that time, the disciples came to Jesus, saying, "Who is the greatest in the kingdom of heaven?" And calling to him a child, he put him in the midst of them and said, "Truly, I say to you, unless you turn and become like children, you will never enter the kingdom of heaven. Whoever humbles himself like this child is the greatest in the kingdom of heaven." (Matthew 18:1–4 ESV)

Young children are humble. They don't carry the cares and burdens we adults do. They don't doubt and second-guess every little thing. They see themselves through their parents' eyes. They accept whatever their parents tell them about who and whose they are. I wished Isaiah could see himself through my eyes and, even better, God's eyes. If he could, then he would have seen the handsome, intelligent, kind, gifted, loving boy the rest of us could see. God could see even more.

I wish I could always approach God as a child. I wish I believed everything He says about me and that I could see myself through His eyes. Being a parent helps me understand a fraction of how God must feel about us. I know He longs for all the same things for Isaiah that I do and much, much more. I always want to believe—and Isaiah to understand—how much God loves him and how he makes Him proud every day. I need to remember that for myself as well—for how God feels about me. And for how I should feel about Isaiah on those days he makes me mad, because one of those days was coming.

CHAPTER 28

MAD

I was finding it difficult to be Isaiah's mom.

I tried to get him up to go to the middle school, but he resisted. One of his classmates had sent me a message the night before, asking if Isaiah could come to school for their yearbook staff picture. He was hesitant to say yes when I asked him about it the night before but agreed to go if he didn't have to see everyone at school. He didn't smile or say good morning to me. He used few words and had a grumpy look and tone the whole time I helped him get ready. I asked him what was wrong, and he said, "Nothing." I accepted that answer and continued to help him, but he was clearly not okay. I asked him again if something was wrong and told him that it certainly seemed like there was.

"You." He looked angry. "I'm mad."

That was interesting since I hadn't had enough time yet that day to do anything to make him mad. "Why are you mad at me?"

He looked even grumpier when he answered. "I don't know."

I told him that if he knew he was mad at me, then he had to know why. "Is it because I take care of you or because I love you too much?"

He didn't seem to know.

"Isaiah, you're not mad at me. You're just mad."

I didn't take it personally, but I did try to figure out where that feeling was coming from as we drove toward the school.

"Are you mad because I help you too much?"

"Yes."

191

That morning, I had tried to help him less, but he asked for help getting dressed and then pouring his cereal. I reminded him that he had asked for help. Then I finally thought to ask, "Are you mad because you need help? Are you mad because you want to be able to do those things by yourself? Are you mad because you can't walk and talk the way you want to?"

His eyes welled up with tears, and he nodded his head yes.

My eyes welled up too. "Are you afraid you'll never walk or talk the way you want to?" Tears came down his face as he nodded his head again. Heartbreak.

"So, Isaiah, you aren't mad at me. You are mad at this situation. It sucks! It does. I know you don't want to go through this. I don't want you to have to go through this either. I hate it for you. You have to be honest with yourself about what you are feeling and know that it's okay to be upset. Everything can't be happy, happy, joy, joy all the time, so cry. You need to cry. Get it out. It's okay. You must know that God is going to work this out. You will recover. You will be fine. You will get through this, and He's going to use your experience to do great things. Do you know that most people never—"

"Mom. Please stop talking."

Okay. So I did.

Yeah, I was rambling, and I forgot he was a boy, and I was using too many words. I wasn't helping him by going on and on. The best way I could help at that point was to shut up and turn the radio on. So I did. He found a song he liked and started to sing along. I had to keep it together because I didn't think it would have helped him to see me cry, but I was so sad. I hated that he was hurting. I hated that he couldn't go to school and be with his friends. I hated a lot about his situation, but there was also so much to love. Aside from the moments of hurt, there had been many more moments of joy. Isaiah could usually find them again quickly. On that day, they came just minutes after the hurts, as we pulled up to the school.

I called his teacher so she knew we were there. I pulled into the school's driveway, turned onto the grass, and headed down the hill toward the back of the building, where we could pull right up to the main door outside her classroom. Isaiah's friend Ryan ran all the way up the hill before we could even drive halfway down, right up to the car. Talk about joy. That kid reached through the window and grabbed Isaiah's hand. "Hey, Isaiah! I missed you, man."

Ryan ran along with the car as we rolled toward where Isaiah's whole yearbook class was waiting outside, waving, jumping up and down, and calling his name. I wasn't sure my heart could take it. Isaiah was all smiles. What a greeting. He loved it.

One of his classmates handed him his yearbook staff hoodie and a T-shirt while I pulled his wheelchair out of the trunk. I had driven Ozzy's car that day because we found that it was easier for Isaiah to get in and out. I rolled it around to his side of the car, but he shook his head no. He wanted to stand. He wanted to be regular Isaiah for those pictures—not the kid in the wheelchair who'd had brain surgery. He put the hoodie on, slowly walked toward the group, and stood in the middle for pictures.

After the group picture, several kids wanted their pictures taken with Isaiah. He put on his cheesiest smile for them. We weren't there long, but long enough for Isaiah's cup to be filled. He enjoyed that short amount of time but was ready to go home. I, on the other hand, did not want to go home. I wanted to be a normal person, too, and go to the store and run errands like normal people do. Isaiah agreed to hang out with me a little longer, so we ran around to a couple of places. His mood was better.

Later, we went to watch Abrianna play basketball. It was a great game, and we had fun. Later, at home, I asked him if he was still mad at me. He said, "No." I told him I don't think he was truly mad at me anyway.

He answered in a soft tone. "No, I wasn't."

We had some tougher than usual moments that day, but I couldn't fully appreciate the good ones if we hadn't had those moments. The situation reminded me of Psalm 30:5 (NLT): For his anger lasts only a moment, but his favor lasts a lifetime! Weeping may last through the night, but joy comes with the morning. (Psalm 30:5) We would continue to find joy in each day, no matter what. We would continue to use those challenging moments as stepping stones toward a greater understanding of our journey. We would continue to find blessings even if they were only in the cracks and crevices of a bad day. Lettie B. Cowman, author of *Streams in the Desert*, once wrote, We look at our burdens and heavy loads, and we shrink from them. But, if we lift them and bind them about our hearts, they become wings, and on them, we can rise and soar toward God.[10] Amen.

The next day went much better. Joy really does come in the morning. It was a therapy day, so we had to get up and get out. Isaiah was in a good mood and ready to work. I realized during the car ride that we hadn't been starting our day with prayer. Isaiah agreed that it was probably the best thing to do each morning. Maybe the previous day would have been better if we had remembered to pray first. When I first started to pray, he watched me to ensure I didn't bow my head and close my eyes while driving. After we both prayed, we turned on some Jesus music and jammed out, singing at the top of our lungs. It was the best ride to therapy ever.

After all the therapy sessions, we had our first family meeting with all the outpatient therapists. My mom participated with Isaiah, Ozzy, and me. The therapists let us know their plans for Isaiah and asked what goals we had.

Isaiah took the floor. "Well," he said. "I can talk. I can talk to . . ." He paused and pointed to me, Ozzy, and my mom. ". . . but I can't talk to people."

We explained that he probably felt more at ease with his family and didn't feel pressure to speak correctly, so he was comfortable speaking around us. He understood.

"And I want to walk."

He let us know he didn't think he'd be able to walk on his own by December 25 as he had originally planned, so he said maybe it would

---

10   Lettie B Cowman, *Streams in the Desert: 366 Daily Devotional Readings*, reissue (Zondervan, 2016).

be later. His PT, Shannon, said that based on how well he was doing, she believed he would walk without assistance by that time. His grin said it all. Showing more confidence, he did his best to communicate some things he had been thinking about. When he finished talking and we had all expressed our desire to help him meet his goals, he smiled again and said, "Okay. Thank you." Then he turned his wheelchair around and headed out, singing to himself.

We all sat there looking at each other for a moment, then laughed. He was done with the meeting, so we figured we were too.

Later that night, he and I talked as he was going to bed.

"Mom. Will I walk?"

"You will walk again, Isaiah. I know it seems like it's taking a long time, but pay attention to the things God is teaching you as you wait. Are you worried?"

He said he wasn't worried but that he just wondered. I think it was more than wonder, but that's okay. Isaiah is young and still learning how to trust God. I haven't even mastered that part of my spiritual life. I know it's hard not to worry about the future, but that's where trust comes in. Most of the time, I choose to trust God for my future because worrying feels bad, and I don't like to feel bad. Barbara Johnson said, "Worry is the senseless process of cluttering up tomorrow's opportunities with leftover problems from today." It also increases gray hair, which means more money spent on hair color. I'd like to avoid that.

But worry does get the best of me at times too. When it does, Matthew 6:25–34 (NLT) gives me perspective:

> That is why I tell you not to worry about everyday life—whether you have enough food and drink, or enough clothes to wear. Isn't life more than food, and your body more than clothing? Look at the birds. They don't plant or harvest or store food in barns, for your heavenly Father feeds them. And aren't you far more valuable to him than they are? Can all your worries add a single moment to your life?
>
> And why worry about your clothing? Look at the lilies of the field and how they grow. They don't work or make their

clothing, yet Solomon, in all his glory was not dressed as beautifully as they are. And if God cares so wonderfully for wildflowers that are here today and thrown into the fire tomorrow, he will certainly care for you. Why do you have so little faith?

So don't worry about these things, saying, "What will we eat? What will we drink? What will we wear?" These things dominate the thoughts of unbelievers, but your heavenly Father already knows all your needs. Seek the Kingdom of God above all else, and live righteously, and he will give you everything you need.

So don't worry about tomorrow, for tomorrow will bring its own worries. Today's trouble is enough for today. (Matthew 6:25–34 NLT)

I do my best. I certainly needed that perspective when it came to the mountain of bills coming our way. My constant vigil over Isaiah was changing. It was time to expand my work.

CHAPTER 29

SPILLS AND BILLS

Before Isaiah's incident, I was not only a substitute teacher, I was also working as a part-time professional photographer. I had not been back to either job since September 8. I felt comfortable enough with Isaiah's progress and needed some sense of normalcy—not to mention money—so Ozzy took the day off so I could work. After an early doctor's appointment of my own, I headed to a photoshoot job for the day. It felt strange to work after two and a half months, but it went well.

Meanwhile, Ozzy and Isaiah hung out at the house. Ozzy helped him with his speech therapy homework, played games, and became the latest victim of Isaiah's mad strategic skills. In the afternoon, Isaiah had a minor accident. Overconfident when getting up and walking back to his chair, he somehow fell. He fell on his behind and wasn't hurt, but it scared him. Tears flowed from both Ozzy and Isaiah. Ozzy said it was so hard to see Isaiah cry because he could see how much he wanted to walk but was not ready to do it all the time. Isaiah was impulsive when it came to getting up and moving around. It was something his therapists had warned against since day one. I assumed the scare would slow him down, but apparently, it didn't—as I would find out later.

Isaiah, Abrianna, and I went to see *Mockingjay—Part 2* with friends that night. Once inside the theater, Isaiah wheeled himself to the bottom of the steps, then stood up. I stayed right behind him as he ascended the stairs. I told him to slow down, but he kept a fast pace. He found the row we would sit in, scooted toward the middle seat, then sat down.

I wanted to smack him upside the head. Instead, I reprimanded him through gritted teeth. "Did you learn nothing from your fall today? Slow. Down."

"Yes."

I gave him a short lecture about his safety that I'm sure went in one ear and out the other.

About a minute later, he said, "Mom, I have to pee."

Seriously? Could he not have thought about that as we wheeled past the bathrooms? So we took the opportunity to practice descending the stairs. I considered scheduling an appointment with my cardiologist as I was certain I would have a mild heart attack before the night was over. Isaiah can be very hardheaded when it comes to doing things on his own. I understood his need for independence, but it might kill us both. I made a mental note to discuss it with him the next day.

I understood that part of it was being thirteen. I was sure that even after his recovery, other situations would threaten his safety. That's the not-so-pleasant part of parenthood. Our kids don't understand how they are wrapped up in our hearts. That's why I continued to pray for strength. I couldn't do this on my own. I couldn't do it with just a little help from my friends. I needed supernatural help. First Peter 5:10 says, And the God of all grace, who called you to His eternal glory in Christ, after you have suffered a little while, will himself restore you and make you strong, firm and steadfast. (1 Peter 5:10) Thank God for that. I need all the strength I can get.

You will be pleased to know I did not have a heart attack before morning. The next day felt like an ordinary day. At least it was our new kind of ordinary. We remembered to start the day with prayer. The more we started each day with prayer, the more Isaiah felt that tug to listen to music that talks about Jesus. It was a pleasant way to enter the first hours of each day before we headed out. That day, Isaiah had therapy.

Moments after we parked in the rehab parking lot, we heard a knock on the passenger-side window. We looked up and saw Carey from the RCP rehab hospital. The look on Isaiah's face was priceless. Pure joy. He opened the door and reached out with both arms, giving her a big hug. She told him how much she missed him.

He smiled big. "I missed you too."

The cardiologist couldn't have prescribed anything better.

The next day was Saturday. Hallelujah! It was the one day of the week we could usually sleep in and relax. On Saturday, we didn't get to sleep in long, but that was okay with me. Isaiah and I headed to our church, where they were holding a yard sale for us. Bills from brain surgery and six weeks of hospitalization were coming in, and the numbers were daunting. We were grateful to our church family and community for helping us bear the burden. It was a gorgeous fall day, and lots of people came. A handful of Isaiah's middle school teachers came to see him and show their support. It felt great to have a kid whose teachers liked him.

From there, we headed to Olivia's basketball game. I loved to watch her play. The joy in my heart was profound as I watched her living inside what had always been our normal. After the game, our friend Philip took Isaiah to the court and encouraged him to practice shooting. Isaiah tried from different angles. He started to get frustrated and tried to sit down. His game wasn't the same with one hand. But Philip wouldn't let him give up. Finally, almost in slow motion, he shot the ball up into the air and watched as it sank into the basket. The crowd went crazy! Well, not exactly a crowd, but a few of our church-family friends. I was thankful for friends who encouraged Isaiah to do normal things and didn't treat him much differently than they did before.

After the game, we all went home, and I took a long nap. I don't know what anyone else in our family did, but I was thankful they let me sleep. Before I drifted off, I felt the full emotion of gratitude as I thought back to the basketball court. I have no idea what I dreamed about, but if I could guess, I would say it was Isaiah playing in the basketball game of his life—running up and down the court and shooting baskets. And Ozzy and me clapping and cheering from the stands.

Lord, show us your healing.

CHAPTER 30

TETHERED

This is the day the Lord has made. I will rejoice and be glad in it even though we had a rough start. Neither Isaiah nor I wanted to get out of bed. Everyone else seemed fine. I heard him say from his room that he wasn't going to church. In all that kid's thirteen-and-a-half years, I had never heard him say he wasn't going to church. I walked into his room.

"Really, Isaiah? You're not going to church?"

"Yes, I'm going." His eyes were still closed.

He finally got up, showered, and then dressed. We were all late, but we made it. It was the Sunday before Thanksgiving—the time of year we think about all we are thankful for and probably thank God more than we do any other time of the year. That year, more than at any other time before, I was aware of my gratitude.

It started with a communion message that touched me. Our friend Yves was speaking, and he talked about being tethered to God. A tether is a cord, fixture, or flexible attachment that anchors something movable to a reference point that may be fixed or moving. I got it. If it weren't for me being firmly tethered to my Lord and Savior, I would not have made it through those previous two-and-a-half months. He is my anchor. He is why I didn't drift off into the land of despair. For that, I am deeply thankful. Romans 8:18 (NLT) says, Yet what we suffer now is nothing compared to the glory he will reveal to us later. (Romans 8:18 NLT) The chapter continues by explaining that one day God will reveal who His children are and that creation "will join God's children in glorious freedom from death and decay" (v. 21). You see, there is so much more to our existence than the suffering we go through. God's full glory will be revealed to us one day. We just have to hang on.

I thanked the Lord in advance for that hope. In Hebrew, the word for that kind of thanks and praise is *towdah*. I encourage you to read the whole inspiring eighth chapter of Romans so you can *towdah* Him for that hope too.

Shortly after the communion message were the announcements. Our friend Philip stood up and talked about the amazing yard sale the church had held for us the previous day. He then announced the total amount raised. Ozzy and I were both moved to tears, overwhelmed by the generosity of our church family, friends, and strangers. I've mentioned before that I'm not a big fan of crying, but that message seemed to release the hounds. When I thought of the ways God was blessing us, I couldn't help but cry. He works through his people, but I know to praise God from whom all blessings flow.

And Isaiah had thought he wasn't coming to church. What he would have missed!

Finally, our minister, Matt Atnip, began his message with a quote from Thomas Aquinas:

> For You supply us all with temporal goods.
> You reserve for us an eternal good.
> You inspire us with the beauty of creation.
> You appeal to us with the mercy of redemption.
> You promise us blessings in reward.
> For all these I am incapable of sufficient praise.[11]

That last line—"For all these I am incapable of sufficient praise"—got me. More tears. Those words were exactly how I felt. I couldn't thank or praise God enough for what He had done. I could only inadequately offer tears of thanks. As I listened to Matt's message, my mind

---

11   Thomas Aquinas, et al, *The Aquinas Prayer Book: The Prayers and Hymns of St. Thomas Aquinas*, reprint (Sophia Institute Press, 2000).

made a list of all I had to be thankful for. It never ends. Each of us has innumerable things to be grateful for every day, but we often don't pay attention until something big happens.

At least that's how it goes for me. He got my attention.

Isaiah and I talked about it on our way home. We talked about the incredible generosity of so many people the day before, we talked about our church family, and then I asked him what he was thankful for. He said, "Mommy, Daddy, Abrianna, and even Olivia." I told him I was thankful for him and his life, then asked if he was thankful for the same.

"Yes. I am a miracle." Then he put his head on my shoulder and a smile on his face, then closed his eyes for a quick nap.

He *is* a miracle, and I am thankful not only for him but also for the rest of my family. I am richly blessed. Isaiah 12:4–5 (NLT) wraps it up quite nicely for me:

> In that wonderful day you will sing: "Thank the Lord! Praise his name! Tell the nations what he has done. Let them know how mighty he is! Sing to the Lord, for he has done wonderful things. Make known his praise around the world." (Isaiah 12:4–5 NLT)

―〰―

On our way to therapy the next day, Isaiah and I had a disagreement about music. I had been quite generous with him as I allowed him to turn on the Christmas music station when we were in the car even though we had a whole month before Christmas. But that day, I had to draw the line at "The Christmas Shoes." I'm sorry, but I refuse to listen to that song. It must be the most depressing Christmas song ever written—a song about a little boy buying shoes for his dying mother so she would look nice for Jesus. I couldn't do it. I changed the station, and Isaiah changed it back. We went back and forth for a while, and then I had to threaten him. I explained how depressing the song was, and he said he wanted to hear it. But my line was drawn, and I wasn't changing my mind. I may have been tethered to Jesus, but no part of me was tethered to that song. He finally let it go, and we listened to another station until we got to therapy.

Later that evening, Ozzy and I had the opportunity to speak to our Wednesday night Bible class about thankfulness. We recounted some of what we had gone through the night of September 8 and shared how we were thankful even amid this huge trial. I realized halfway through Ozzy's portion of the talk that we had failed to prepare Isaiah for what we were going to say. We shared some raw emotions about everything we had been through. At one point, I looked at Isaiah, and tears were streaming down his face. About the same time, my mom laid her eyes on Isaiah and saw his sweet face melting and felt he needed her, so she went and sat next to him, wrapping her arms around him. I wanted to melt down myself.

Isaiah was emotional through most of it. He had never heard the things we shared. Some of his friends and Abrianna showed up and surrounded him, also giving him comfort as he listened to the words we spoke. When class was over, I went to him and told him I was sorry we didn't prepare him for what we talked about and that I could see it was difficult.

He smiled. "That's okay. I didn't cry."

I raised an eyebrow at him.

"Okay, I cried once."

Right. Once. Then he put the brakes on his wheelchair, stood up, and gave me a giant bear hug. That boy. He knows how to get me.

Later, I asked him what the hardest part to hear was, and he said, "Abuelita."

Ozzy had talked about how even though Isaiah lived through surgery on the eighth, we still had to get through September 9. As I mentioned before, that was the date of his mom's birth and the day she died three years back. We could have lost our son on the exact date we lost his mother. Isaiah didn't know that part of the story. I asked him if there was anything else.

"You prayed for me."

I had assumed he knew I prayed for him during all that, but I guess he never really thought about it. I think it was hard for him to hear the words I used as I pleaded with God to spare his life. It was probably a good thing for him to hear some of what we went through that September. He will hear and understand more as time goes on.

The next day was Thanksgiving, and we had so much to be thankful for. That year, I was most grateful for the lives of my children. As parents, we know we are connected to our children, but I'm not sure we can completely comprehend how strong that bond is until something happens to threaten that connection. Imagine how it must affect God. He not only created us, but He gave us our very lives. Whether we choose to acknowledge it or not, that tether is strong.

I prayed that we would all wake up in the morning with thanks and praise on our lips, if for no other reason than having the knowledge that our Creator loves us more than we could possibly imagine.

CHAPTER 31

LEVELING UP

Thank you, Lord, for the sun. After enduring such dreary weather for so many weeks, I was extra thankful for the clear, sunny days we were having. This particular day was the kind of day I couldn't help but smile at, which was a good thing, because early that Saturday morning, we were awakened by our smoke detector screaming, "Fire!" Only it wasn't fire. It was smoking bacon that Ozzy was cooking for our family and visiting cousins Sal, Jessica, Ilan, and Juju. What a way to be woken up on a day we could sleep in!

My heart started beating again, and I took in a whiff of thick, greasy, bubbling bacon. Breakfast had been cooked and was waiting for us. I wasn't ready to get up, but I was able to go back to sleep with a smile on my face, knowing what would be waiting for me when I woke up the second time.

We all took our time getting ready for the day and decided to head downtown. Greenville has a picturesque park right in the center of downtown. It even has a suspension bridge stretched out over a gorgeous waterfall. Because it was such a beautiful day, many people had come out, and visitors had taken the parking spots near the park. So Isaiah needed to use his wheelchair instead of the walker as he had wanted. It was too far for him. I pulled his wheelchair out of the trunk and placed it by his side of the car. He was terribly upset about it. I apologized to him but also told him he needed to use the chair. He agreed to sit, and then he pouted about it the whole way to the park until I finally asked him if he wanted to get up and push me in the chair. A huge smile came across his face, and he said yes. So we switched places.

We got some funny looks as I think people could tell that maybe Isaiah was the one who should be in the chair, not the lady holding her purse on her lap. I'm pretty sure they weren't thinking I was mother-of-the-year material, but Isaiah was happy. And I think it was good for him—I had an ulterior motive anyway. He pushed for about ten minutes or so, then finally said, "Okay, Mom, I'm tired."

Mission accomplished! We switched places and went on our way. I did have to point out that he would have been so much more tired, without any relief, if he had brought only the walker. We enjoyed the park for a while, took some pictures, then headed out to have one last meal with our cousins and in-laws, including Eddie, Sandee, and their kids, Elijah, Mateo, and Aaliyah, who had joined us at the park.

Apparently, Isaiah was ready to get up and walk again, so he and Sandee changed places this time. She was amused by the looks people gave as Isaiah pushed her up the sidewalk. We landed at a pizza place, The Mellow Mushroom. Much of the time, we played the game *Telephone*, with one person sending a message around the table person by person and having it end up a jumbled mess of words. Isaiah struggled to understand the whispered words. We somewhat remedied that by having the person who whispered to him sing the message to him instead. As we had learned in the hospital, the singing and speaking parts of our brains are different. So we had been using melodic intonation therapy to help him with his speech. Words and phrases that Isaiah had a hard time speaking were a snap for him to sing. It helped him with the game too, and we had a great time.

Spending time with people you love provides a good dose of joy, and it's free. I was reminded on days like that how important it is to smile and laugh. Proverbs 15:15 (NLT) says, For the despondent, every day brings trouble; for the happy heart, life is a continual feast. (Proverbs 15:15 NLT) And in her book *Choose Joy*, Kay Warren wrote:

Laughter and tears come from the same deep well in the soul. That's why sometimes we laugh until we cry, and sometimes we cry until we laugh. . . . God intends for you to be able to weep freely and laugh uproariously, just as Jesus did. When you can recognize both the pain and the humor around you, you take another step toward knowing true joy.[12]

It was a good day. We were leveling up in many ways—especially joy. And the next day, I knew I would have another kind of gladness, waking with the words of the psalmist in my heart: I was glad when they said to me, "Let us go to the house of the Lord." (Psalm 122:1 NLT)

Sundays became even more precious because I loved having that time to worship with fellow believers. I found I was happier on those days. I guess when your universe shifts and changes your perspective, that's the kind of thing that happens.

After church, we went to my parents' house to eat Thanksgiving leftovers. While we were there, Isaiah needed lots of extra hugs. I asked him why he was so cuddly.

"Because you're so soft."

I mean, I am a soft woman—but he meant that the shirt I had on was soft. It really was. I made a mental note to remember to wear that shirt anytime I needed extra affection.

Later that evening, Isaiah was bound and determined to do yoga exercises. "I want to yoga," he declared.

"No. You need to wait for Shannon to tell you what workout you can do." He had done some yoga before, but she had told him he could damage his shoulder if he did something during yoga that pulled his arm in a harmful way.

He didn't care. "I have to yoga."

"No, you don't, son. You can wait one more day and ask Shannon what other workouts she has for you to do."

He insisted. "I have to yoga, Mom. I have to get my fat."

---

12   Kay Warren, *Choose Joy: Because Happiness Isn't Enough Choose Joy* (Echristian, 2012).

His weight had become an ongoing issue. He would tell me he was fat and then want to exercise or eat a certain way. One day he asked me if he could run up and down the stairs. I wasn't sure he was still connected to reality, so I was glad we were going to meet with the psychologist the next day.

That night, I decided to make soup for dinner. It was a late dinner because I'd been occupied most of the afternoon. I hadn't made a meal in a while because so many friends had been gracious to help, so Isaiah wasn't used to me being unavailable while I cooked. From the time I started to the time I finished, he called for me every five minutes, asking me for help with something. Ozzy had gone to the store, so he couldn't help. Not that it would have mattered, because like most kids, Isaiah thought his mom was the answer to every problem. We had been doing so well, but that night I stressed and slightly panicked. *Here it is. This is what I was worried about. I'm not going to be able to do anything normal. He needs me every second. I don't think I can handle this.* I was close to tears.

I realized Isaiah would have to learn to wait, and if I thought about it, there were plenty of times he didn't need me. I knew I would be able to make a meal. I knew it would be okay, but I still felt unsettled and upset. Then the Word spoke to me: The Lord will guide you continually, giving you water when you are dry and restoring your strength. You will be like a well-watered garden, like an ever-flowing spring. (Isaiah 58:11 NLT) I could rest in the Lord.

Anyone bearing the title Mom can find encouragement through God's Word to get through each day. I should probably write this verse on my forehead: He will feed his flock like a shepherd. He will carry the lambs in his arms, holding them close to his heart. He will gently lead the mother sheep with their young. (Isaiah 40:11 NLT)

Oh Lord, lead away, because we have a long way to go. And the road before us is steep and long.

CHAPTER 32

SEASON OF OVERWHELM

Mondays were packed from morning till night. As we did every week, we began with therapy. We talked to Shannon about Isaiah's desire to do yoga and other workouts. She set aside what she had planned to do and sat down with him to search for a yoga video that would work for his stage of recovery.

I appreciated that she listened to him even though they ended up unable to find one she approved of. He would have to be patient and do the exercises she gave him until he was ready. But Isaiah had developed an extreme stubbornness. Once he put his mind to something, it had become difficult to talk him out of it. He would not accept no as an answer. That could have been a good quality in some arenas, but I didn't like this circus where he went around and around with his mother. We needed to work on that.

After those long Mondays, Tuesday was our day to sleep in and rest. Isaiah was able to sleep until he was completely ready to get up. He needed that. I spent most of the day trying to clean and juggle all the tasks on my to-do list.

The stress of the season had begun. There were presents to buy. There were Christmas parties, Christmas concerts, Christmas plays, Christmas cookies, Christmas decorations, Christmas cards, teacher gifts, and that stinkin' Elf on the Shelf! It was all quite overwhelming. I was apprehensive about managing money during a time when finances were tight. Even more so, I felt I wasn't creating enough memories. I think that concern is common among women. We presume we are responsible for everything. I have a helpful, supportive husband, and I still struggle with that. I can't imagine what my single mom friends go through. Many people say I seem calm, cool, and collected all the time, but I'm not. I worry the same way everyone else does, but I usually talk and pray myself through it.

And here we were again with me thinking I was in charge of all the small stuff. Maybe I'm subconsciously under the illusion that because it's so small, I shouldn't bother God with it. When I think about my problem that way, it's silly. As a parent, I want my kids to come to me with even their minor problems. God loves me even more than I love my kids, so why would I think He wouldn't want me to come to Him with even the small things?

How do I know He cares about the seemingly insignificant things? Because Luke 12:7 (NLT) says, And the very hairs on your head are all numbered. So don't be afraid; you are more valuable to God than a whole flock of sparrows. (Luke 12:7 NLT) If I can trust God with my child's life, I can trust Him to guide me to the best memory-making experiences for my children. I can trust Him to help me get my mind together to manage my time better. I think if I asked Him, He would probably throw me a good Elf on the Shelf idea. There are problems I struggle through and can't seem to find a resolution for, then realize I didn't even talk to God about them. When I finally present it all to Him, my load immediately becomes lighter, and then I wonder why in the world I didn't talk to Him sooner. Sometimes it simply takes the problem leaving my lips.

God's Word is also a healing balm we can use when it's difficult to trust Him. I often struggle so much to trust Him that I say, "I trust you God, I trust you God, I trust you God," over and over until I truly do. It works. And so does reciting these verses:

> Give all your worries and cares to God, for he cares about you. (1 Peter 5:7 NLT)

> Do not be afraid or discouraged, for the Lord will personally go ahead of you. He will be with you; he will neither fail you nor abandon you. (Deuteronomy 31:8 NLT)

Give your burdens to the Lord, and he will take care of you.
(Psalm 55:22 NLT)

I try not to beat myself up because I worry sometimes. Some people say that as believers we should never struggle with worry. But we are *human* believers, and God gets it. He understands because He made us, which is one of the reasons He gave us His Word—to remind us that He is here for us.

I said a prayer that God would help me through my anxiety, then headed downstairs to move that stinkin' elf.

The next day was a rainy, sleepy day. Isaiah and I both had a hard time staying awake at therapy. Even though he was tired, he still worked hard and made lots of funny hard-work faces. He even walked better than I had seen him walk in a long time.

It was also one of those days that had me flashing back to the night Isaiah went to the hospital. I felt many different emotions at once. Mostly, I felt the fear of almost losing him, as well as the extreme joy of still getting to be with him here on earth. Both feelings had me weepy. The weight of the emotions overwhelmed me, yet part of it was gratitude. We'd had no time to decorate—except for that doggone elf who managed to sneak back into our house—so the full force of holiday cheer was delayed. But what a special holiday season it was for our family.

I had a feeling I would experience that tug from both sides of our situation for the remainder of the year. And that feeling made me weepy too.

Isaiah had been fun and giggly for a couple of days. Every day—at least ten times—he pretended he was falling. He thought it was hilarious. I thought it was funny simply because he cracked up every time I looked at him. He didn't care how many times I didn't fall for his joke—he was going to keep trying. I figured I would have to tell him "The Boy Who Cried Wolf" story again.

That afternoon after picking up Olivia from school, we stopped to drop something off for my friend Sylvia at her house. I left Isaiah and Olivia in the car because I didn't plan to be long, but I stayed talking with her longer than I thought. After a while, she looked up at the door with a shocked look on her face. Isaiah was standing there. He had taken a not-so-short walk from the car to her door without a walker or anything.

She opened the door, grabbed him, then wrapped her arms tightly around him. I thought she might never let go. She cried big tears. It was a precious sight. It was a gift for Sylvia because she worried so much about him, and to see him standing there at her door was really something. It was a God thing. She was having a tough time and needed that "hug from God." It's amazing how God works through us, even when we have no idea what He's doing until it's over. Sometimes we need a sign that God is still there, loving and caring for us.

And there I was again, remembering the year of dryness before September 8, the year feeling God was not around or simply not speaking to me. I know God is always here, but sometimes I don't feel Him. I'm sure it has more to do with my state of mind and heart than it does His actual presence. God gets it though. David, who was one of God's "favorites," wrote these feelings out in Psalm 13 (NLT):

> O Lord, how long will you forget me? Forever?
> How long will you look the other way?
> How long must I struggle with anguish in my soul,
> with sorrow in my heart every day?
> How long will my enemy have the upper hand?
> Turn and answer me, O Lord my God!
> Restore the sparkle to my eyes, or I will die.
> Don't let my enemies gloat, saying, "We have defeated him!"
> Don't let them rejoice at my downfall.
> But I trust in your unfailing love.
> I will rejoice because you have rescued me.
> I will sing to the Lord
> because he is good to me. (Psalm 13 NLT)

David poured his heart out in anguish, but at the end of the day, he still knew God was there, God loved him, and God was good. I love that psalm. It's so real.

I encourage those of you struggling with life and struggling to believe that God loves you and is still present in your life to get on your knees—get on your face even—and pour your heart out to Him. Scream, yell, cry, and tell Him how angry you are—whatever you think you need to do to communicate how you feel. God understands. He already knows every part of you, but He wants you to talk to Him and get the words out. Then when you're done, get up, wipe your tears, and tell Him that you trust Him. If you don't, then say it over and over until you do. It may take some time, but don't give up. He'll never give up on you.

You might want to go in the closet. You don't want to scare the children.

The next day was a day off for Isaiah, so he could sleep in. I, on the other hand, had stuff to do. I took a short nap in the morning, but I think I dreamed of all the tasks I still had to do. At 11:33 a.m. I remembered that Isaiah had a dentist appointment at noon. I went into panic mode and told him I'm sorry I forgot about his appointment, but we had to go. He wasn't fully dressed, so I ran upstairs and grabbed some clothes and practically threw them at him, then ran back up to get myself ready. When I came back down, he had put on his jeans and a jacket over the shirt he had on already and that he had worn all day the day before.

Um, no. I told him to take it off because it was probably funky and to put on the shirt I had given him. He didn't want to wear the shirt I gave him, and I didn't want to argue, so I ran back upstairs and grabbed a shirt I knew he would like, then ran back downstairs. He took off his jacket and his funky shirt, and I put the new one on him. I told him he would have to let me help him put his shirt on because we were in a hurry. He complied. I also helped him get his shoes and socks on. We headed out the door and made it to the dentist by 12:01 p.m.

We rock.

Isaiah's teeth looked good. No cavities. Wow. Hallelujah. His teeth were hardly ever brushed in the hospital—it was the last thing on my mind. I chalked this great report up to supernatural cleanliness.

We spent the rest of the afternoon running around. Again.

That night was Abrianna's second basketball game of the week. Oh. My. Goodness. It was crazy. I must admit I was screaming right along with my crazy New Yorker husband and my referee/coach-in-training son. Isaiah was so upset with the refs at one point that he stood up to go home. How in the world did he think he would get there? Another time, he looked at one of them and said, "You're a bad ref."

I had to stop him and explain that yelling about a bad call is one thing, but a personal comment like that is not okay. I understood how he felt because I wanted to yell the same thing, but that's just rude. Not that all our previous yelling wasn't, but you have to draw the line somewhere.

I'm not sure games like that were good for Isaiah because he was spent by the time we arrived home. I could tell his brain function was on the slower side. I decided that next time, I would take him home early. I loved how much he wanted to support his sister, but I wasn't sure how much he could take. Her team's loss hit him harder than it should have.

Once we were home, I realized that Isaiah still had homework to finish, and I needed to help him. I had a ten-year-old wanting to read with me before bed, a fourteen-year-old basketball player in a lousy mood whom I wanted to comfort, my room to clean, a Facebook update post to write, a dog who kept getting in my face asking me for something (which I didn't understand because I don't speak dog), and a stinkin' elf to move.

Wait a minute. Where was Ozzy? I felt completely overwhelmed and wanted to crawl into bed and hide. Instead, I walked away from the dog, began helping Isaiah, and asked Ozzy to read to Olivia. When Ozzy was done with that, I asked him to take over helping Isaiah. Isaiah was having such a hard time understanding some of the things he usually does well with. His brain had had too much stimulation that day, and because I was feeling overwhelmed, I struggled to be patient with him, so I was glad Ozzy could do it. I went upstairs, prayed with Olivia, talked briefly to Abrianna, who just wanted to go to sleep, then sat down to start typing an update for my Facebook page. I felt calmer. Writing has therapeutic qualities.

In that writing experience, I was reminded that much of what we struggle with each day has deeper roots than we often realize. Paul says, For we are not fighting against flesh-and-blood enemies, but against evil rulers and authorities of the unseen world, against mighty powers in this dark world, and against evil spirits in the heavenly places. (Ephesians 6:12 NLT) Right. The authorities of the unseen world win when I can see only the struggle of the day or the season. My difficulties had been only part of my day, so I chose not to allow the last hour or two to define the whole thing. I knew they, too, would pass. I planned to wake up the next morning in recognition of a brand-new day, complete with brand-new opportunities to honor God. His mercies are new every morning.

CHAPTER 33

THE TRUMPET'S CALL

I had *planned* to wake up that Friday morning fresh and recognize the opportunities of the day, but Isaiah and I both battled fatigue. God's mercies are new every morning, but not every morning brings renewal. Another patient we had gotten to know at therapy told me that I never looked tired, but I sure did that day. It's going to sound ridiculous, but it wasn't until that day I realized how much all of this was to deal with. I mean, I always knew what we were going through was a lot, but it was really *a lot*.

After therapy, we enjoyed a lovely lunch with a good friend. Then we ran back and forth, picking up and dropping off the girls. I took Abrianna to another facility for a PT appointment. Yes, another child who needed PT. We found out she had a labral impingement of the hip. She would need therapy twice a week. While sitting there watching her get evaluated that afternoon, I felt overwhelmed again.

So now I have to keep up with therapy for two kids? Really? God, please help Abrianna be self-motivated to do the exercises she has to do to get better. Please don't make me have to beg and plead with her to do them every day. I can't. I'm too tired.

I ended the day feeling defeated and in a not-so-great mood. I know I was allowed a bad mood once in a while, but I didn't like it. I looked for a show on Netflix to fall asleep to, have a good night's sleep, then wake up and start all over again. I knew that everything would be fine, and peace would come again.

That night I meditated on James 1:2–4 (NLT) once again because it always gives me perspective:

> Dear brothers and sisters, when troubles of any kind come your way, consider it an opportunity for great joy. For you know that when your faith is tested, your endurance has a chance to grow. So let it grow, for when your endurance is fully developed, you will be perfect and complete, needing nothing. (James 1:2–4 NLT)

I felt somewhat better Saturday, although I spent that whole morning in bed. I snoozed on and off, trying to catch up on sleep. Isaiah came in a few times to check on me. At one point, he crawled in bed with me, wrapped his arms around me, and snuggled in.

"You're so cuddly, Mommy."

He's such a sweet boy. That time together reminded me of when he was a baby, and I would lie in bed with him, my arms wrapped around his whole little body like a teddy bear and go to sleep—except this time it was his arms around me. He did this two or three times throughout the morning. He told me I needed to get up. I guess he was worried, but I told him I needed to rest and I would get up later. I told him to go hang out with his dad.

I did eventually get up around lunchtime. I ate breakfast, had a cup of coffee, and then started to work on the Christmas decorations. I felt better, but I probably lacked Vitamin D, so I started taking it again. Living in a hospital room under artificial lights for six weeks had depleted me of many nutrients, I'm sure. I needed to take better care of myself. It was my birthday week, so I decided to focus more on *me* that week.

At some point that afternoon, I heard a familiar sound—one I hadn't heard in months. It was Isaiah blowing on his trumpet. He had tried a few times before but got frustrated and stopped. That day was different. I heard the notes travel up and down the scales. I ran into his room. "Isaiah, I heard you! You're doing it! You're playing your trumpet!"

He looked at me with a half-grin and said, "But it's not good."

I assured him that it was amazing compared to the last time he had tried. He played it again. That time was even better. I watched as his left hand gripped the trumpet and his fingers wrapped around the brass tube to push down on the valves. All trumpets are played with the right hand regardless of which hand is dominant. Trumpets are made for the right hand. Isaiah was going to teach himself how to play with his left hand. He would have to adjust everything. But I believed he would do it, and we would see a miracle.

When Ozzy came back home from picking Olivia up from a sleepover, I told him what Isaiah had done, and I asked him to do it again for his dad. I knew it would be quite a task, but my skin was tingling as I anticipated hearing him play once more. Isaiah loved playing the trumpet even more than playing football. He played it again, and that time it was twice as smooth and precise as it was before—what a gift! It had been heartbreaking for me to see his disappointment over not being able to play, so hearing him blow that horn made my heart sing. I praised God for His marvelous gifts, focusing on Psalm 150.

> Praise the Lord.
> Praise God in his sanctuary;
> praise him in his mighty heavens.
> Praise him for his acts of power;
> praise him for his surpassing greatness.
> Praise him with the sounding of the trumpet,
> praise him with the harp and lyre,
> praise him with timbrel and dancing,
> praise him with the strings and pipe,
> praise him with the clash of cymbals,
> praise him with resounding cymbals.
> Let everything that has breath praise the Lord.
> Praise the Lord. (Psalm 150)

Then I thought of the Scripture passage that tells the story of the Pharisees trying to get Jesus to silence the whole crowd of disciples who were praising God joyfully for all the miracles they had seen. "I tell you," he replied, "If they keep quiet, the stones will cry out." (Luke 19:40)

The Lord will be praised no matter what. Isaiah will not be silenced. Maybe Satan intended this whole thing for evil, but the Lord meant it for good (Genesis 50:20). Thank you, Lord.

—∾—

Though Christmastime tended to be stressful for me, Sundays did not fall into that category. That time of year, Sundays are particularly special. It seems that every minister begins December by focusing on the anticipation of the birth of Christ. When the congregation sings, there appears to be more joy behind every expression of song. That Sunday was no exception. Even though Christ's birth happened over 2000 years ago, the weeks before Christmas evoke the same kind of anticipation in me even today. I think part of the story for me is hope.

Along with the birth of Christ came real hope. I carry deep within me the anticipation of being with Him in heaven one day. No matter what happens in this world, I carry within me the hope that came with the birth of a precious baby boy.

I have hope because of Jesus. I know that no matter what I go through, I have a hope in Christ that trumps it all. That is truly the foundation of why I could be so strong through all of Isaiah's trials. There's a bigger picture. This world is not all there is. Isaiah knew it too. God has offered his gift: the greatest expression of love possible. And we've gladly received it.

There was a prophet named Simeon who waited with great anticipation for the birth of the Messiah. He was told he would not die until he laid eyes on Jesus. Can you imagine how he must have felt when he finally saw that baby? Oh my goodness, I think I would have passed out from the overwhelming amount of joy. Once He saw Jesus, he essentially said, "Okay. I can die now." All because love became a man.

Monday came around again, and it was as busy as usual. I'm guessing that this particular Monday was Isaiah's favorite day of therapy so far. He enjoyed cooking breakfast as his OT and part of PT. He had planned his menu last week, and today he made eggs, bacon, and pumpkin pancakes. He did a fantastic job. He was having so much fun that he would break into song and dance while cooking. Then he would stop and say, "*Mmm.* Oh yeah. So good." The aroma around the rehab facility was heavenly. He made plenty of pancakes so the staff could enjoy them. And he received many compliments on his cooking skills.

Isaiah had become antsy about walking and doing things on his own. He rarely used his wheelchair anymore and seemed resentful even toward his walker. The issue was that he had to strap his right hand to it before walking, then unstrap it before sitting down. I understood. It was a tedious task. He would often take off and start walking. He could do it. The problem was his impulsivity, which made walking unsafe. He still needed support. Shannon told him that once he received his orthotic brace, walking would become much safer. That news made him laugh and do another little dance. He knew that he would reach his December 25 goal. He might even beat it.

Strange though it may seem, I realized Isaiah laughed more now than he did before his brain injury. His laugh had changed though. He sounded like a different person. Well, he was a different person. He was enlightened. He was experienced. He was challenged. He was also bossy, stubborn, and a know-it-all. But some things hadn't changed. He was still cuddly, lovable, sweet, and sensitive. And when someone complimented him, he was still quick to toot his own horn in agreement.

I liked this new Isaiah just as I had liked the earlier version. So I prayed he would be walking on his own by December 25—and that the laughter would continue.

CHAPTER 34

GOLD-PLATED SNEAKERS

Isaiah was only two weeks from the goal date of walking on his own, so it was perfect that he had an appointment to see Dr. Troup. I always looked forward to seeing him because he is a real hero—at least to my family and me (I'm sure many other families are also still together because of him). That day he had news for us I never expected. He told us that the bleeding on Isaiah's brain had nothing to do with football and that it had been caused by an arterio venous malformation (AVM). AVM is a congenital disease in which there is a tangle of arteries and veins due to weak arterial muscle. Isaiah had probably experienced an increase in blood pressure that caused it to rupture.

I asked him if Isaiah could play football again. He said yes. As long as Isaiah's right side fully recovered to do what he needed to do on the field, he could play. Talk about a happy boy. I don't think Isaiah understood fully what Dr. Troup was saying until I explained it to him once we were in the car.

He cheered. "Yes! I can hit!" He was over the moon.

Dr. Troup had explained to me that football could be the carrot we dangled in front of Isaiah to motivate him to do his best to recover fully, and it did motivate him. I know you're wondering how I felt about that. Well, I decided that if God chose to bring him complete recovery and Isaiah wanted to play again, I would not stop him. Ozzy thought the same. We would spend whatever was necessary to get him the best and safest helmet we could find, and then we'd have to let it go in God's hands. I must trust that if God took care of Isaiah through

WHEN GOD CHANGED HIS MIND

so much, He would continue to do so. I also trusted Dr. Troup, and if he said that football was not the cause of what happened to Isaiah, I believed him. I said before that I would not let Isaiah go back to football, but something was telling me it would be okay. He probably wouldn't be able to go back to it anyway. If he didn't completely recover his vision, he wouldn't be an effective linebacker. I trusted God to handle it. I would not worry about tomorrow. Tomorrow has enough worries of its own.

After seeing Dr. Troup, we headed to my friend Chris's house, where a few of my girlfriends gathered for some fellowship. Isaiah made a face when I first told him he'd have to hang with a bunch of older women, but he seemed to fit right in and even provided comic relief. On our way home, about two minutes after we got in the car, he said, "That was fun." Isaiah can make the best of any situation, even if that means hanging out with a bunch of "old ladies."

Even so, I realized the next day that I had run him around too much the day before, and he started the day already tired. He was sluggish in speech therapy and struggled through OT—it may have been the most challenging day he'd ever had in OT. He kept laying his head down on the table and sighing, and he had a difficult time completing the tasks his therapist Shannon (yes, another therapist with the same name) set before him. Some days, he had no choice but to wake up and push himself. And if he wanted to make his walking and speaking deadlines, this was one of those days.

So after therapy, we went to a store and walked around. He rarely used the wheelchair anymore, only the walker. I tried to give him as many opportunities to walk as I could. As we shopped, I thought about buying him a pair of gold-plated sneakers for Christmas since it would be such a monumental day in more ways than one. I even thought about adding wings.

That night at church was bring-your-parent night for the youth. Ozzy and I sat behind Abrianna and Isaiah as we worshiped and listened to their youth minister, Charlie, who talked about what he had prayed for and ultimately learned throughout that year. He then encouraged each of us to reflect on our year and what God had done in our lives. Unlike most years, I didn't need time to think. I already knew. A lot had happened and changed for our family. I know I can speak for Ozzy when I say that he and I were stretched beyond anything we'd ever experienced before.

We then sang one of my favorite songs, "Oceans" by Hillsong United. I sang the words, asking the Lord to lead me to a place of boundless trust. That was what I had desired and prayed for over a long period of time. That's exactly where God had led me over those previous three months. I asked him to take me places that would allow my faith to grow stronger in His presence.

The next day was my birthday. I had made plans to go out with friends that night. I wasn't looking forward to it, but I was trying to be a normal person. Thankfully, as the day neared, my enthusiasm was working its way from somewhere down around the soles of my shoes right on up to the top of my smiling face.

The downside was that I would miss Isaiah's band concert, which I hadn't thought a big deal since he couldn't play anyway. But Isaiah had been reminding me for several weeks that the concert was coming up on December 10. He made sure I knew he wanted to be there. At the beginning of the week, he had reminded me again, saying how pumped he was to go and watch his friends play. I asked if he were a bit sad as well. He said he was. Isaiah was a part of the advanced band (eighth grade) as well as the wind ensemble. This year, Isaiah had made first chair and was extremely disappointed he could not fill that seat. I admired him for still wanting to be there to support his friends.

So as I got ready to go out, Isaiah prepared to see his friends perform. He put on his tux, complete with his award-medal-clad cummerbund (his wind ensemble uniform). Such a handsome boy. I felt torn because I wanted to be there for him. The night could still tear up his emotions. But I needed to have some time for me too, and I knew for certain I would get emotional being there and mourning that particular loss. I needed to laugh and enjoy my birthday, not weep over what Isaiah was unable to do. I kissed Isaiah and the rest of my family goodbye and headed out. He was in good hands with his dad. His Nani and Papa would also be there.

Ozzy was asleep when I got home, but I woke him up because I wanted to hear all about the concert. He had a break in his voice as he described the night. He explained the bizarre feeling he'd had as they walked in and through the crowd. Everyone was looking at them. Of course, they were! They were watching a living, breathing, walking miracle.

As I looked through the pictures Ozzy had taken, my eyes welled up with tears. It was beautiful to see the joy in my boy's eyes and not-so-crooked smile. Tears escaped from my eyes when I watched a video another band mom had posted of the wind ensemble playing a beautiful piece. Isaiah sat there in the front row, fully immersed in the music floating around him and soaking it all in. It was difficult for me to see him sitting there in the "wrong" seat just listening.

I also watched a video of his band director, Jim Kilgus, saying kind words about Isaiah. He then walked over to give Isaiah what can only be described as one of the most genuinely love-filled embraces I have ever seen, followed by a standing ovation from the whole wind ensemble, and, I am guessing, the crowd around them.

Jim Kilgus is an extraordinary man. He loves what he does, and it shows. He inspires kids who have never picked up an instrument before to learn, practice, and play the most beautiful music you could imagine coming from such young students. He not only has a gift, but he *is* such a gift to so many, and Isaiah adores him. If you know someone who loves your child and inspires them to be great, you know how I feel about Jim.

Ozzy said that on their way home, he had asked Isaiah if he felt emotional. Isaiah said, "No, just happy." I prayed that our boy could get back to doing what he loved very soon. I prayed that God would accelerate his healing so that he could pick up that trumpet with his right hand and play his little heart out. Then I allowed the tears to flow freely. With every ounce of salty emotion coming out, bits of peace flowed in. I remembered the apostle Paul's words in 1 Thessalonians:

Rejoice always, pray continually, give thanks in all circumstances; for this is God's will for you in Christ Jesus. (1 Thessalonians5:16–18) So I thanked the Lord for every part of the journey.

I was still emotional in the morning. I knew God had big plans for Isaiah. My prayer was that I didn't ruin him in the meantime. I'm kidding, but don't parents feel like that sometimes? You have a great kid(s), and you earnestly pray that you don't screw them up. That's why we need Jesus.

And, Jesus, we've got just two weeks to go.

CHAPTER 35

ANTICIPATION

I t was the middle of December, seventy-five degrees, and gorgeous. Olivia had a basketball game that day and the whole family attended. Isaiah and Abrianna had a lot to say from the bleachers. When the youngest in the family plays a sport, she has many coaches.

Later, the kids and I attended the Nutcracker Tea put on by the English Theatre Arts Dance Company. When our friend Liz invited the girls to go a couple of weeks before, Isaiah caught wind of it and said he wanted to go too. The boy is quite cultured. On our way, we picked up his aunt Sandee and cousin Aaliyah. I did warn him ahead of time that it would be mostly girls. He looked at me and shrugged his shoulders. It was a lovely event, complete with tea, little sandwiches, and petite desserts. Liz's daughter Sarah (my child whom I didn't give birth to and other people are raising) played four roles in the ballet. Isaiah loved every minute of it.

That night, before he went to bed, we hung out in my room. I could tell something was on his mind.

His countenance changed, and the corners of his mouth pointed downward. "I want my hand."

"What do you want to do with it?"

"Play my trumpet."

He explained that he wanted to use his right hand the way he uses his left. He felt especially down about it that night. Maybe he'd been thinking about it since the band concert. He missed playing with his friends. He missed Mr. Kilgus. They were his people. I told him that he would get his groove back. It would just take time.

Earlier that evening while at dinner, I had reminded him of an intense therapy program in San Diego that PT Shannon had strongly recommended. Isaiah told me he didn't want to go. He didn't want to fly. He had only been on a plane once in his life when he was a baby, so he didn't remember, and he was afraid.

I understood that the thought of getting on a plane that ascends thousands of feet into the sky was terrifying to him. But I tried again. "The therapy will help you get your hand back, Isaiah. That's what it's for."

"Really? Okay! I'll go."

"Yeah, you will."

But his voice still slumped when he said a few minutes later, "I can't use my hand. I can't feel my foot."

It was difficult to hear him say that. I didn't have any kind of inspirational speech prepared. He had mostly been so strong, brave, and positive. Watching him work through those tough moments when he became so aware of his new reality—it hurt me too.

I said all I knew to say. "I'm sorry. It will get better." I reminded him that he needed to work on therapy even at home and continue working hard every day. When I went to his room later to pray with him before he went to sleep, I asked him how he was feeling.

"Feeling?"

"Yeah. Are you happy, sad, frustrated, or mad?"

"No."

"Are you just blah?"

"Yeah. Blah."

I nodded. "Well, I love you, and I'm thankful for you," I said, then hugged his scarred head.

He smiled. "Miracle."

"Yeah, but I was thankful for you even before your miracle."

He smiled, and we prayed. When we finished, I told him good-night, hugged him, and gave him a kiss.

"My baby," he said.

I explained to him that I am not his baby. He is my baby and always will be.

He grinned. "But I'm bigger than you."

"I don't care how big you get. You will *always* be my baby. Always. Goodnight."

Our bond had grown so much stronger since our experience together in the hospital. I knew that thirteen was that age he should have been bonding with his dad, and I felt some guilt about it, but I continued to hold on to those precious moments. I knew it wouldn't always be that way.

We were trying to get back to normal yet knew nothing would ever be the same. Each day brought more insight. I sang with the praise team at church for the first time in months. It felt amazing. Joy overcame me while we sang about baby Jesus and His mother, Mary. I had never considered much about Mary's emotions as a mother before. I could sing "Mary, Did You Know?" without an ounce of empathy. That year, it hit me differently. I had come close enough to losing a son to comprehend how it might feel. Of course, I'm not comparing myself to Mary or Isaiah to Jesus, but I can understand being the mother of an extraordinary boy—a boy who was impacting so many, whom I have the blessing and honor of calling my son. I also felt the overwhelming responsibility to train him in the way he must go (Proverbs 22:6) so he would be equipped for what God had planned for him. When God changed His mind the night of September 8, it changed everything. I can now picture Isaiah grown up, with a family and a job, full of life, and thriving. The feeling I would lose him one day had gone away. That feeling has been replaced with a more profound sense of joy and hope for the future.

The story of Abraham and Isaac comes to mind. That life-changing night, I truly had to give Isaiah over to God—to sacrifice him in a way. I knew that God could save him, but I didn't know if He would. There it is again: *I know He can, but will He?* That night I had to open the grip I had on my son and present him to the Lord, trusting God to do what He knew was best. And like the ram He provided to take the place of Isaac on the altar, He provided healing for Isaiah. This December day of worship was yet another day full of reminders of how gracious God has been to our family.

> Oh, how my soul praises the Lord.
> How my spirit rejoices in God my Savior!
> For he took notice of his lowly servant girl,
> and from now on all generations will call me blessed.
> For the Mighty One is holy,
> and he has done great things for me.
> He shows mercy from generation to generation
> to all who fear him.
> His mighty arm has done tremendous things!
> He has scattered the proud and haughty ones.
> He has brought down princes from their thrones
> and exalted the humble.
> He has filled the hungry with good things
> and sent the rich away with empty hands.
> He has helped his servant Israel
> and remembered to be merciful.
> For he made this promise to our ancestors,
> to Abraham and his children forever. (Luke 1:46–55 NLT)

The next day during therapy, I had to get firm with Isaiah a couple of times when he tried to lie down and nap, but he listened, straightened up, and got to work. I told him he had better sit up and work hard if he wanted to play football. Talk about motivation.

Later, I took him and Abrianna shopping. Isaiah was a perfect companion for her, giving his opinion on clothes he thought would look nice on her. They talked and laughed together as they walked around the store—such a sweet and annoying sight. Shopping with two teenagers can be torturous. I'm reasonably sure they were laughing at me at one point. That's okay though. It was worth seeing the camaraderie. We stopped at one more store before Isaiah hit a wall. His feet hurt, and he was exhausted. We went home after that, but it was much later than planned.

At home, Isaiah was solemn. He came upstairs where I was writing and lay down on our bed. I asked him if he were okay.

"I want to go to the hospital."

"Why, Isaiah?"

"I just want to go."

"You miss it?"

He covered his eyes with his forearm—the functional one. "Yes."

"What do you miss?"

"Everything," he said somewhat defiantly.

We talked about his feelings some more, and it came down to that he missed the routine of therapy every day. He was frustrated because he felt that his recovery had slowed down. He was sad because he couldn't move his hand, leg, foot, or face the way he wanted.

"Isaiah, I'm so sorry you feel sad. It's okay to be sad. It's okay not to be happy all the time."

I think he *was* happy most of the time. Still, nights like that, when he was so exhausted that the simple things—the things he used to do with no problem and now on a good day struggled to do—became increasingly difficult, and he experienced frustration like never before. I reminded him that when people ask him how he is doing, he doesn't have to say good, as he always does. I tease him about the way he says it. He says it in his I'm-fine-I'm-great-everything-is-wonderful voice. Remember how Jim Carey says, "It's good!" in the movie *Bruce Almighty*? That's how Isaiah says it. I laugh every time, but it's not reality.

I let him know that when people ask him how he's doing, it's okay to say, *Eh, I'm okay*, or *I'm frustrated today, but it will get better*, or something like that. I reminded him of the amazing things that had happened and promised him I would show him pictures of what he was doing (or not doing) in September so he could see how far he had come.

Maybe nights of aggravation like that one were good for him on occasion because they lit a fire under him to work harder at his recovery.

His dejection tugged at me, but I reminded him as well as myself that God's not done with him yet. I reminded him that our God is bigger than all of it, and He would take care of him. Isaiah's countenance seemed better. He woke up and went to take a shower, which—by the way—he could do all by himself. Ozzy and I found it amusing that Isaiah's view on personal hygiene had changed so much. He used to tell us that his funk smelled good because it meant that he smelled like a man. I guess his nose had finally joined the rest of us in the land of reality. For that, we were truly thankful.

After he finished showering, he asked me to pray with him, and we talked a little more. I reminded him that in only a few days, my sister Victoria and her husband, Eric, would be there as well as my brother Anthony. I may have done a little dance when I said, "Our whole family will be here." That gave him a big smile. Family makes everything better. Well—a *good* family makes everything better. I reminded him of how loved he is by so many people and that God was still working everything out.

I asked him again, "How do you feel?"

"Sad."

"About what exactly?"

"Everything," he said, in no particular tone.

I looked down to pick up pieces of my heart that had crumbled to the floor. "It's going to be okay," I promised. "You will get better." I kissed him goodnight, then went back to my room.

Those emotional nights were tough, but I knew they were normal, and the next day he would probably wake up with a new perspective. He usually did. Exhaustion is a thief that can steal hope. But it can't keep hold of it if we don't let it. I, for one, was eagerly awaiting Christmas Day and being home with my whole family. We were blessed beyond belief, and I refused to allow hopelessness to creep in. God is good. All the time.

> Therefore we do not lose heart. Though outwardly we are wasting away, yet inwardly we are being renewed day by day. For our light and momentary troubles are achieving for us an eternal glory that

far outweighs them all. So we fix our eyes not on what is seen, but on what is unseen, since what is seen is temporary, but what is unseen is eternal. (2 Corinthians 4:16–18)

CHAPTER 36

DANCING IN THE RAIN

Vivian Greene said, "Life isn't about waiting for the storm to pass, it's learning to dance in the rain." That's how Isaiah lived this December day. A few times a year, my friend Sylvia, some ladies from church, and I prepare a luncheon for the ladies at Miracle Hill Renewal Center. I usually bring along the girls, but this time Abrianna decided to go to her sister's basketball game, and Isaiah wanted to come with me. As soon as we stepped inside, he wanted to help. One of the ladies opened the door to a storage area and pulled out a table to set up. Isaiah hobbled over to her, grabbed one end of the table with his left hand, and helped her pull it out. Of course, I had a minor internal freak-out as I pictured him being pulled by the weight of the table and falling over. I'm sure I had that crazy-mom look on my face when I said, "Isaiah!"

"Mom. I got it," he assured me.

I tightened my lips together, looked at Sylvia, who also looked concerned, and said a little prayer to myself as he stood at one end of the table opposite the woman, then flipped it over with one hand. Good grief, he was strong! He was totally in his element. He wanted to help, and he was beaming. Yes, he definitely had it.

I grabbed a tablecloth to put on the table, and he helped with that too. He continued to help me as I decorated the tables. He did a lot of it on his own. Finished with the tables, we went into the kitchen to see how we could help the ladies there. I hung out there for a while, not noticing when Isaiah walked out.

Several minutes later, Sylvia appeared in the kitchen and said, "Christina, you have got to come see Isaiah. He is cutting up with these women."

I walked into the family room and watched Isaiah holding the hand of an older woman, dancing to Christmas music.

He was dancing.

They both had big smiles on their faces, as did all the women standing and sitting around them. They didn't know his story. They didn't know how he had cheated death and was a dancing miracle right in front of their eyes. He didn't know their stories either. He didn't know that he was dancing with a recovering drug addict. He had no idea how that one dance probably encouraged that woman's very soul. What a sight. Isaiah had found his happy place again, as well as his dancing feet.

> You have turned my mourning into joyful dancing. You have taken away my clothes of mourning and clothed me with joy, that I might sing praises to you and not be silent. O Lord my God, I will give you thanks forever! (Psalm 30:11–12 NLT)

This season! The air outside had settled in at lukewarm—nothing like I thought it should be at Christmastime, but it still felt like Christmas to me. I was thankful for all the ways God continued to bless us, so I was full of holiday cheer. I grew up in California and had this kind of Christmas weather every year until I was fifteen. I just had to get the kids to buy into it. I thought maybe I'd turn the AC down to fifty degrees. Maybe that would help.

Cheer infused Isaiah again. It was Christmas cheer but really so much more. We went out to lunch with good friends and laughed a lot. Isaiah was visibly happy, dancing in his chair a lot of the time. After we finished eating, he asked to go home and rest. When we got back, he went straight to his room and took a nap. *Who is this kid?* But he had decided that no exhaustion was going to steal his hope or joy as it had that recent night.

The next night was our Holy Night program at church. It meant so much more that year as we celebrated life and love.

September 8 had indeed been such a holy night. God was present in that room where we prayed and waited with our "framily." God was present in the operating room, guiding Dr. Troup's hands as he saved Isaiah's life. God was present when I texted a group of friends, "I'm in a nightmare." God was present in my sense of peace, in the knowledge that God was with us, in the knowing that no matter what happened, Isaiah—and we—would be okay. Whether he went to be with Jesus or was allowed to stay with us, we would be okay. That right there is supernatural—peace in the middle of a nightmare. That's why September 8 was a holy night. As we, along with thirty-two of our closest friends, gathered in that small waiting room and called on our Creator with absolute desperation, the ground beneath our feet became holy.

So this night, as we sang, "Fall on your knees, O hear the angels' voices, O night divine," I knew I had been to that place before—on my knees.

At the end of the program, Santa made an appearance. That big boy of mine sat right up on Santa's lap to take a picture. He delighted in things he had been too cool for before. I loved the change. Somehow he had regained some of his childlike wonder.

Isaiah was making progress, too, as he practiced his trumpet. He was determined to get it back. It had to be difficult to learn how to play on a nondominant hand, much less on the opposite hand he'd initially learned. And walking—he wasn't 100 percent yet, but close enough to be proud of his progress. As I had often been doing, I took some time to read to him the comments people made on our Facebook page. That night, after I had read four or five, he said, "Too much happy." He wanted me to stop. It made him emotional, so he was having trouble hearing those words, though I knew he would be ready to read them himself one day.

It was easy for me to find joy during that time because all I had to do was look at my children. I was still aware that Christmastime can be difficult for so many. There has been so much loss, so much pain and hurt among God's children. I was grateful for what I had but felt the pain of those around me who had lost so much.

The only way I can wrap my head around the pain is to remember that we live in a fallen world and evil roams this earth. Events of struggle or loss often cause people to lose their faith and sometimes to find it. Even in the most difficult of situations, I know God can be glorified. I don't believe He makes these things happen. He allows them to happen.

Sometimes people do horrible things to other people. God has gifted each of us with free will. Free will is both a gift and a curse. Sometimes I wish I didn't have it. Sometimes I wish I was a beautifully perfect robot who did everything right, always made good choices, and never suffered consequences because of poor choices. And if everyone were this kind of robot, then nothing bad would ever happen because we would all make the right choices.

If that were the case, what would be the point of existing? If everything were perfect, our highs wouldn't really be highs because we wouldn't know the difference without having experienced the lows. So with that perspective, I accept my free will. With that perspective, I accept the free will of others. With that perspective, I accept that bad things happen to good people. It's nothing God *ever* intended for His children—but truly, He loved us enough to give us free will. Free will to love Him. Free will to reject Him. Free will to birth life. Free will to take it away.

So what do we do with all the excrement we are left with on this earth? We use it to fertilize the garden we choose to grow. If we sow love, peace, and forgiveness, we will reap the same. We work harder to love, even when it is just plain hard.

I struggle with a kind of survivor's guilt—not so much *guilt*, but the question of *why* my son, my baby, was allowed to live, and others are not. Why do so many other mothers' sons die but mine didn't? I can look only to my faith. I think God *allows* bad things to happen because from His vantage point, He sees things we never will. I know through my family's struggles, lives have been changed. I would never have asked for this, but I am truly thankful for my son's life. My son's now-difficult life has made a difference.

A friend told me that although she does not share my belief system, she is glad I find comfort in it. The truth is, it is not *just* comfort I find in it. I find peace. I find joy. I find hope. I can't think of anything we need more today. Paul's words in Romans capture my thoughts:

> Because of our faith, Christ has brought us into this place of undeserved privilege where we now stand, and we confidently and joyfully look forward to sharing God's glory. . . . And this hope will not lead to disappointment. For we know how dearly God loves us because he has given us the Holy Spirit to fill our hearts with his love. (Romans 5:2, 5 NLT)

Joanna Weaver's writing does too. We were not created for this earth alone, but for an infinite future with God. A destiny beyond the realm of mere time and space. How would our lives change if we truly woke up to that reality?[13] I don't wonder why this medical event happened to Isaiah. I know that God did not create him *for* this, but I know He will do mighty things with all Isaiah has been through.

From our side of heaven, we see how God not only changed His mind, we see how Isaiah has been changed. From God's side, He's always known Isaiah's purpose and where He would take him. The supernatural change we witnessed was for building our faith, along with a glimpse into God's character. It was all a part of His plan to grow each of us in ways that bring Him glory. I no longer fear losing Isaiah, though I know tomorrow is not promised to any of us. I rest in knowing I can trust our Creator in every area of our lives, even if it leads to death.

---

13   Joanna Weaver, *Lazarus Awakening: Finding Your Place in the Heart of God* (WaterBrook Press, 2011).

CHAPTER 37

HE'S ALWAYS THERE

Merry Christmas!

The kids said this was their best Christmas ever. After opening gifts, we hurried over to an assisted living facility to meet our friends, Emmy and Yvonne, along with my sister Victoria and her husband, Eric. Emmy started a ministry several years ago called Project Christmas, and we'd been doing it with them for a few years. We spent time with the residents singing Christmas carols, visiting, and passing out cards and gifts. As we were getting ready to leave, Isaiah spotted a woman trying to get down the hall in a wheelchair by herself. So he abandoned his walker and walked over to her.

"Can I push you?"

She was thrilled. She said yes, and off they went. Although his act of kindness deeply moved me, I was also concerned. How was he going to push her when he had such limited control of his right hand? He had pushed Sandee and me that one day downtown, but this was a stranger. What if he accidentally pushed her into a wall? Well, I don't know how he did it so well, but he pushed her chair with both hands down the hall and into the dining room, where he tucked her chair neatly in place at a dining table. I think everyone's heart melted right then and there. I tried to hand him his walker back when his task was complete, but he refused it. He was done. It was Christmas Day, and he would walk on his own. He was ready. The walker had just been a safety net.

After our lovely visit with the residents, we headed home to finish wrapping presents for our extended family. Then we drove over to my parents' house for gifts and gumbo. My mom makes the best gumbo ever. We had a family Christmas tradition to go to the movies on Christmas night. So we went to see *Star Wars: The Force Awakens*—all fourteen of us. Family. We were super nerdy and wore our Star Wars shirts.

The day after Christmas was full of more family, friends, and reflection. The family sat around having a conversation with our friend Kendra about our experience in the hospital.

Isaiah said with a puzzled look on his face, "But, Mom, you weren't there."

I thought he was joking. I chuckled. "Whatever, Isaiah."

"What? Papa and Nani were there, and Dad was there, and Charlie came, but not you."

I was floored and hurt. I proceeded to have a temper tantrum—I mean, a rational conversation. "You have got to be kidding me. I was there every single day. I fed you, slept right next to you every night, and I even wiped your butt!"

Kendra was sympathetic. "Don't feel bad. You were part of his daily surroundings, and you probably blended in like medical equipment."

I thought about her words for a minute and calmed down. But seriously. How could he not remember the times I fed him, clothed him, cleaned him up, and comforted him when he cried? I was there every minute.

Oh wow, I realized. *Isn't that kind of like our relationship with God?* He is *always* there taking care of our daily needs, but somehow we forget—on the days we think we need Him—that He has never left. He is a permanent fixture we ignore until our needs become "bigger" or more evident. Then we invite Him to be a part of our lives. We invite Him to carry away our troubles. But don't you know, He's been there the whole time. The whole time.

Maybe today, you can stop, look around, and *see* Him. If, for some reason, you can't see Him, then *seek* Him. I promise He is there feeding you, clothing you, wrapping His arms around you when you cry. Feel His presence.

When you take time to recognize Him, you'll see. Maybe He was that friend (or even stranger) who was there when you needed someone to talk to. Perhaps he was that person who smiled at you in the grocery line. Maybe He was the doctor who delivered much better news than you expected or the person who gave you hope and comfort after receiving devastating news. Perhaps He was the tiny little flower that miraculously shot up in the crack of the sidewalk you were walking on or the magnificent rainbow glowing through the dark clouds after a storm. He tells us in Isaiah 41:10 (ESV), "Fear not, for I am with you; be not dismayed, for I am your God; I will strengthen you, I will help you, I will uphold you with my righteous right hand."

Don't you know how much He loves you? He knows you by name, and He is with you. There is nothing you can do to change His love for you. Think about the worst thing you've ever done. Guess what? He *still* loves you. He is patiently waiting for you to acknowledge Him. Those bad things that are happening to you are not his form of punishment. He didn't *do* that to you. Those things come from the evil one. The Lord is still waiting for you to fall into His arms of love and acceptance. Nothing can separate you from that. This God I know—this God that's bigger than it all—is the God of Revelation 21:

> Then I saw a new heaven and a new earth, for the old heaven and the old earth had disappeared. And the sea was also gone and I saw the holy city, the New Jerusalem, coming down from God out of heaven like a bride beautifully dressed for her husband. I heard a loud shout from the throne, saying, "Look, God's home is now among his people! He will live with them, and they will be his people. God himself will be with them. He will wipe every tear from their eyes, and there will be no more death or sorrow or crying or pain. All these things are gone forever." (Revelation 21:1–4 NLT)

It thrills me to no end, living in the knowledge that this life is temporary. If you could see my smile at this very moment as I remind you that the struggles we go through on this earth are temporary, you would know—we were created for eternity.

There the Lord is waiting for you. And He won't change His mind.

EPILOGUE

saiah gave a brilliant and inspiring sermon one week after his birthday. He received an overwhelming standing ovation. The emotion rendered me hardly able to stand. He went on to star as the king in his middle school's performance of *Cinderella*. He memorized and sang all his lines with perfection. He received another standing ovation as he took a bow at the end of the show. He graduated from high school with honors in the class of 2020—a year that will never be forgotten.

Today, six years after his brain bleed, Isaiah is finishing his sophomore year in college. He has come as far as we hoped. He still walks with a leg brace and a limp, has limited use of his right hand, and has no peripheral vision to the right. But he drives his own car, camps and hikes with friends, plays sports, and refuses to let any disability stop him from doing what he wants. And that shake the medical team promised he would have if he didn't take the medication was gone just a few months after we got home.

Isaiah is studying kinesiology to become a physical therapist and has recently felt God calling him to add public speaking to his studies.

When asked if it upsets him that he lost some of his physical abilities, he responded, "It's been hard, but it's okay that this happened to me. I'm thankful that I'm alive. I'm learning a lot, and I still have a lot of joy."